John Kootas

OXFORD WORLD'S CLASSICS

THE COMPLETE ODES

PINDAR lived in the Boeotian city of Thebes, about 40 miles north-west of Athens. Born in 518 BC (he died some time after 446) and a contemporary of the tragedian Aeschylus, he lived during the Persian Wars and subsequent growth of the Athenian empire, and was ranked in antiquity as Greece's greatest lyric poet. What we know about him is mostly derived from his poetry itself. He is most famous for his epinician or victory odes, composed for winners in the ancient athletics festivals and sung to music by a chorus. His patrons included the Sicilian tyrants Hieron I and Theron, Arcesilas IV king of Cyrene, Megacles uncle of Pericles, and a number of other wealthy and powerful families who commissioned odes from him, but he was on particularly friendly terms with victors from the island of Aegina, for whom a quarter of the forty-five surviving odes were written. He wrote many other poems, for both states and individuals, but all of these survive only in fragments.

ANTHONY VERITY was formerly Headmaster of Leeds Grammar School and Master of Dulwich College. In his retirement he acts as an educational consultant. He has translated Theocritus' *Idylls* for Oxford World's Classics.

STEPHEN INSTONE is an Honorary Research Fellow at University College London.

OXFORD WORLD'S CLASSICS

*For over 100 years Oxford World's Classics have brought
readers closer to the world's great literature. Now with over 700
titles—from the 4,000-year-old myths of Mesopotamia to the
twentieth century's greatest novels—the series makes available
lesser-known as well as celebrated writing.*

*The pocket-sized hardbacks of the early years contained
introductions by Virginia Woolf, T. S. Eliot, Graham Greene,
and other literary figures which enriched the experience of reading.
Today the series is recognized for its fine scholarship and
reliability in texts that span world literature, drama and poetry,
religion, philosophy and politics. Each edition includes perceptive
commentary and essential background information to meet the
changing needs of readers.*

OXFORD WORLD'S CLASSICS

——

PINDAR

The Complete Odes

——

Translated by
ANTHONY VERITY

With an Introduction and Notes by
STEPHEN INSTONE

OXFORD
UNIVERSITY PRESS

OXFORD
UNIVERSITY PRESS

Great Clarendon Street, Oxford OX2 6DP

Oxford University Press is a department of the University of Oxford.
It furthers the University's objective of excellence in research, scholarship,
and education by publishing worldwide in

Oxford New York

Auckland Cape Town Dar es Salaam Hong Kong Karachi
Kuala Lumpur Madrid Melbourne Mexico City Nairobi
New Delhi Shanghai Taipei Toronto

With offices in

Argentina Austria Brazil Chile Czech Republic France Greece
Guatemala Hungary Italy Japan Poland Portugal Singapore
South Korea Switzerland Thailand Turkey Ukraine Vietnam

Oxford is a registered trade mark of Oxford University Press
in the UK and in certain other countries

Published in the United States
by Oxford University Press Inc., New York

Translation © Anthony Verity 2007
Editorial material © Steven Instone 2007

British Library Cataloguing in Publication Data

Data available

Library of Congress Cataloging in Publication Data

Pindar.
[Works. English. 2007]
The complete odes / Pindar; translated by Anthony Verity; with an introduction
and notes by Stephen Instone.
p. cm.—(Oxford world's classics)
Includes bibliographical references.
ISBN–13: 978–0–19–280553–9 (alk. paper)
1. Pindar—Translations into English. 2. Laudatory poetry, Greek—Translations into English.
3. Athletics—Greece—Poetry. 4. Games—Greece—Poetry. I. Verity, Anthony. II. Instone, Stephen. III. Title.
PA4275.E5P3 2007   885′.0109—dc22   2006039673

ISBN 978–0–19–955390–7

1

Typeset by Cepha Imaging Private Ltd., Bangalore, India
Printed in Great Britain
on acid-free paper by
Clays Ltd, St Ives plc

CONTENTS

THE ODES

OLYMPIANS

PYTHIANS

Contents

NEMEANS

ISTHMIANS

INTRODUCTION

Pindar's Odes

The victory ('epinician') odes of Pindar (518–*c*.438 BC) celebrate athletes victorious in the ancient games. Pindar did not invent this type of poetry—the lyric poets Ibycus (sixth century) and Simonides (*c*.556–466) had composed poems celebrating athletics victors, of which fragments survive;[1] Bacchylides, Simonides' nephew and Pindar's contemporary, also composed them, and thanks to papyrus discoveries fourteen of his victory odes now exist in varying degrees of completeness.[2] But Pindar perfected the genre and forty-four of his victory odes survive in their entirety, and, whereas Bacchylides' odes were virtually completely lost until their rediscovery on papyrus in 1896, Pindar's odes were handed down through the ages in a continuous manuscript tradition; they alone, therefore, of ancient Greek victory odes were an influence on the form of the ode in Renaissance poetry.[3]

Most, but not all, of the odes follow a typical pattern and contain standard ingredients: direct praise of the victor and his home town, general moralizing, a myth about gods and heroes that has been tailored to be relevant to the victor, something about the performance of the ode and the poet himself. The mythical section is often the main part of the ode, and Pindar liked if possible to draw on myths connected with the victor's home town, some of which may have pre-existed as local stories. He was also influenced, both for myths and moral sentiments, by earlier epic poetry, especially Homer's *Iliad*, Hesiod (not only his *Theogony* and *Works and Days*, which survive in their entirety, but also other now fragmentary Hesiodic poetry, for example *Catalogue of Women* and *Precepts of Chiron*) and the body of post-Homeric epic known as the 'epic cycle'.[4]

---

[1] See M. L. West (ed.), *Greek Lyric Poetry* (Oxford, 1995), 97 (Frag. S 166) and 160–1.

[2] For translations of Bacchylides, see vol. iv of the Loeb series *Greek Lyric*, ed. D. Campbell (Cambridge, Mass., and London, 1992).

[3] See 'Pindar's Influence' below.

[4] For the influence of the *Iliad*, see notes on *Olympians* 7.18 'island of three cities', 9.76 'Thetis' son', 13.60 'Glaucus', *Pythian* 3.80 'for every blessing . . . a double grief ', 3.112 'Nestor . . . Lycian Sarpedon', *Nemean* 2.13–14 'Salamis . . . Hector . . . Ajax'; for Hesiod and Hesiodic poetry, see on *Olympian* 9.41–2 'Protogeneia's city', *Pythian* 1.17 'Typhos', 6.22

Victory odes belong to the genre of Greek poetry known as 'choral lyric' because they were sung by a chorus of singers to musical accompaniment on a special public occasion. The other type of Greek lyric poetry is the more personal lyric which the poet sang solo to an informal gathering, represented by Archilochus, Sappho, and Anacreon for example.[5] This type of lyric poetry also influenced Pindar: he puts seemingly personal statements into the odes; some of the odes are short and 'monostrophic' (with a single, repeated stanza) like much personal lyric; at the start of *Olympian* 9 he attributes to Archilochus an informal refrain sung to victorious athletes and contrasts this with his own victory ode; he himself also composed personal poetry, his 'encomia'.[6]

Pindar was paid for his victory odes, and several times alludes to the fact that the recipient of the ode is paying for the fame bestowed on him.[7] It is possible to connect the origins of the victory ode with the existence in Greece of powerful individuals who entered the major games not merely to win but also to increase their fame and standing, and employed poets such as Pindar to publicize their achievements. Ibycus lived at the court of Polycrates, tyrant of Samos, and Simonides was not only encouraged by Hipparchus, son of the Athenian tyrant Pisistratus, but also celebrated a mule-race victory of Anaxilas, tyrant of Rhegium.[8] Pindar composed some of his most famous poems for the Sicilian tyrants Hieron and Theron.[9] These tyrants lived in a dangerous world, beset by critics and plotters; they paid their poets not only to praise their achievements but also for political advice, since Greek poets, divinely inspired by the Muses, were traditionally

---

'Philyra's son', 9.13 'Hypseus . . . king of the haughty Lapiths', *Nemean* 4.56 'Peleus', *Isthmian* 6.35 'Aeacus' son', 6.67 'Hesiod's maxim'; for the epic cycle, see on *Olympian* 13.53 'Medea', *Pythian* 6.22 'Philyra's son', *Nemean* 10.56 'Therapne'. Translations of fragments of the epic cycle are in the Loeb series *Greek Epic Fragments*, ed. M. L. West (Cambridge, Mass., and London, 2003).

[5] Translations of these authors can be found in West (ed.), *Greek Lyric Poetry*.

[6] Translations of surviving fragments can be found in the Loeb edition of Pindar by W. H. Race (Cambridge, Mass., and London, 1997), ii. 346–59.

[7] Cf. *Pythian* 1.90: 'if it pleases you to hear that men always speak well of you | do not grow weary of spending', and the last sentence of *Isthmian* 1: 'If a man keeps his wealth hidden indoors . . . he does not realize | that he will pay his soul to Hades unattended by fame.'

[8] West (ed.), *Greek Lyric Poetry*, 160 (Frag. 515).

[9] *Olympians* 1–3, *Pythians* 1–3. Simonides and Aeschylus also stayed with Hieron, cf. *Olympian* 1.10–17 'the rich and blessed hearth of Hieron . . . His glory gleams in the best of poetry and music, | of the kind that we men often compose in play | at his hospitable table.'

regarded as repositories of wisdom. In his odes for the Sicilian tyrants Pindar mixes praise with political advice, and offers through the myths examples both to follow and to avoid (kindly Croesus and sadistic Phalaris at the end of *Pythian* 1, for example). Pindar's longest victory ode by far (*Pythian* 4) is for Arcesilas, king of the Greek colony Cyrene in north Africa; Pindar also composed *Pythian* 5 for him, the first lines of which celebrate the power of wealth, and he composed *Pythian* 9 for a victor from Cyrene. Some other odes, too, are for victors from Greek colonies or victors who had moved to new cities. Such people, as much as the Greek tyrants, needed to have their positions reinforced, so they too sought victory in the games and victory odes.[10] But Pindar was a realist and well aware of the precarious nature of political power: he lived during the Persian Wars when Xerxes invaded and tried to conquer Greece, he mentions several occasions when Hieron intervened militarily, and he knew the threat posed by the growth of the Athenian empire.[11] Political instability, the fickleness of fortune, and the dangers inherent in power are all themes that play a large part in his odes. There is also an important religious dimension to them: like most Greeks, he thought both that to achieve success one needs the help of the gods and that too much success and prosperity is dangerous and will attract the jealousy of the gods. Pindar's gods included not only the traditional Olympian deities but other lesser divine figures and powers, such as the Graces (see *Olympian* 14) who provide the grace needed for poetry, victory, dancing, and singing; the Seasons (*Olympian* 4); Concord (*Pythian* 8). Many of the heroes and heroines he mentions were descended from gods or goddesses; some of the victors he wrote for traced their ancestry back to heroic figures. Gods and heroes were for the Greeks powerful, living forces which needed to be respected. Some great men were posthumously worshipped as heroes, and a few even when alive.[12] In his odes, Pindar stresses the inevitable gulf between men and gods, but also how the superhuman

[10] Cf. S. Hornblower, *Thucydides and Pindar* (Oxford, 2004), 26–8.

[11] For political and military themes in the odes, see further notes on *Olympian* 12.1 'Zeus the Deliverer', *Pythians* 1.47 'battles', 1.76–7 'Salamis . . . the battles before Cithaeron', 2.18–19 'maiden of Western Locris', *Isthmian* 1.33 'Onchestus', and the headnotes to *Pythians* 7 and 8 and *Isthmians* 5, 6, 7 and 8.

[12] See B. Currie, *Pindar and the Cult of Heroes* (Oxford, 2005). For religious themes in the odes, see also the headnotes to *Olympians* 2 and 3, and on *Olympian* 8.3 'burnt offerings'.

achievement of athletics success in supreme competition can to some extent bridge the gulf.[13]

Pindar

Our main source for what we know about Pindar derives from what survives of his own poetry. But in it he often adopts a persona, so what he appears to say about himself has to be used with caution as biographical evidence. He came from near Thebes, in Boeotia, about 40 miles north-west of Athens, and birthplace of Heracles. In his odes he has a special affection for Heracles, as a proto-athlete from his home city. By and large he keeps his own political views out of the odes, tailoring his opinions to be acceptable to his clients. Even though Thebes and Athens did not always see eye to eye during his lifetime, Pindar still composed odes for Athenians and other poetry for Athens. Sparta gets numerous complimentary references, but this is often simply because it was the birthplace of the Dioscuri, Castor and Polydeuces, great mythological athletes; no ode is for a Spartan, no poem is for Sparta, whose austere environment was not attractive to Pindar. He preferred lavish hospitality, especially that of Aegina, an island south of Athens; on it was (and still is) a famous temple to Aphaea, an Aeginetan goddess similar to Artemis, rebuilt in the early fifth century.[14] Pindar composed nearly a quarter of his odes for Aeginetan victors. He travelled to Sicily and stayed with Hieron,[15] for whom he composed *Olympian* 1 and *Pythians* 1–3 in the 470s. He says he was entertained by Chromius, a general in Hieron's service, for whom he composed *Nemean* 1, probably also in the 470s.[16] In the last sentence of *Pythian* 4 (462) he says that at Thebes he recently entertained Damophilus, an exile from Cyrene, and in the last sentence of *Olympian* 10 (476) he says he saw the victor winning at Olympia.

In the odes, Pindar often combines himself as poet with the chorus that sang the odes on his behalf and functioned as his spokesperson,

[13] Cf. the beginning of *Nemean* 6.

[14] See A. Pippin Burnett, *Pindar's Songs for Young Athletes of Aigina* (Oxford, 2005), 29–44.

[15] Cf. *Olympian* 1.17.

[16] *Nemean* 1.19–22 'I stand singing of noble deeds | at the outer gates of a hospitable man, | where an acceptable feast has been prepared for me'.

playing with the roles of the chorus and himself, with sometimes his own point of view uppermost (as in the proud boast at the end of *Olympian* 1: 'May you walk on high in this reign of yours, | and may I always be the victors' companion, | pre-eminent by my poetry throughout all Hellas'), sometimes that of the chorus (such as the beginning of *Nemean* 9: 'Let us go in revel company . . . Come, fashion a sweet hymn of verses . . . Let us then lift high the deep-voiced lyre | and lift up the pipe' (lines 1–8)). Sometimes poet and chorus fuse together so that the viewpoint is partly that of the poet, partly that of the chorus, and partly an imaginary and fictitious composite one (for example, *Pythian* 5.72–80), just as some of the scenarios represented in the odes are (as when, in the passage referred to from *Nemean* 9, we read 'Let us go in revel company, Muses, | from Apollo's temple at Sicyon to newly founded Aetna', where what is meant is 'let this poem encompass both Sicyon, the venue of victory, and Aetna, the victor's home city'). This explains how Pindar can on occasion readily interchange 'I' (=Pindar) and 'us' (=the chorus), as at the beginning of *Isthmian* 8 (lines 5–11), and makes it difficult to attribute to Pindar with certainty what he may appear to say about himself.

The Games

The victory odes are divided into *Olympians*, *Pythians*, *Nemeans*, and *Isthmians* after the four great 'panhellenic' games that were open to all Greeks. All athletics games in ancient Greece were part of a religious festival in honour of gods or heroes. The Olympic games were the oldest and most prestigious, held in Elis in the western Peloponnese in honour of Zeus. There had been a sanctuary to Zeus there even before the traditional date for the founding of the games (776 BC). Athletics competitions provided an additional way of honouring the god, the winner owing his victory to the help of the god and in consequence thanking the god. The festival lasted five days and took place, as nowadays, every four years. On the first day Zeus *apomuios* or 'averter of flies' was invoked to keep the sacrificial meat fly-free, and on the third day a hundred oxen were sacrificed to Zeus. The programme of events developed and changed during time. In the fifth century, when Pindar was writing, there were three running events: the stadion (a sprint the length of the stadium), the diaulos (there and back), and the dolichos (twelve laps); a race when the runners wore armour and carried a large shield (there and back); boxing, wrestling, and the pancration ('all power', in which virtually any method of physical attack was permitted); the pentathlon (long-jump, sprint, discus, javelin, and wrestling). Most of these events had separate age-categories for men, youths, and boys. There were also horse and horse-with-chariot races held in the hippodrome. For a few Olympics there was a mule race (*Olympian* 6 is for a winner in this event); mules were bred in Sicily, and the Sicilian tyrants may have played a part in establishing this event. The Pythian games were held in honour of Apollo at Delphi. The programme was broadly similar to that of the Olympics, but included music competitions (for Apollo the god of music); *Pythian* 12 is for a winner in the pipe-playing competition. They were traditionally founded in the 580s and like the Olympics held every four years, in the year before the Olympics. The Nemean games, traditionally founded in 573, took place every two years at Nemea on the east of the Peloponnese. They were also in honour of Zeus. The Isthmian games, traditionally founded in 582, also took place every two years. They were held in honour of the sea-god Poseidon at the Isthmus, the strip of land that then connected the Peloponnese with mainland Greece. In his victory odes Pindar generally refers to the god presiding over the games where the victory had been gained, and sometimes the myth relates to the particular games (for example, in *Olympian* 1 the myth concerns Pelops who had a hero-cult at Olympia).

These four games formed a circuit for athletes, as the Olympics, World Championships, European, and Commonwealth Games do for some athletes today. A few outstanding athletes, such as Diagoras of Rhodes for whom Pindar composed *Olympian* 7, won at all four (like the British decathlete Daley Thompson who in the 1980s simultaneously held Olympic, World, Commonwealth, and European titles). In most events the athletes competed naked (probably because of the heat). Several times in his odes for victors from Aegina Pindar praises the trainer.[17] Generally, he concentrates on the implications of victory rather than the winning itself, but occasionally he provides interesting athletics details. In winning at the Olympics both the stadion race and the pentathlon Xenophon of Corinth achieved,

---

[17] *Olympian* 8.54–66, *Nemeans* 4.93–6, 5.48–9, 6.65–6; see also headnotes to *Isthmians* 5 and 6.

according to Pindar, what had never been done before (*Olympian* 13.29–33). In *Pythian* 5 (lines 49–51) Pindar says that the charioteer of the victor, the king of Cyrene, was in a race in which forty charioteers fell. The dangers inherent in the equestrian events meant that the men who entered those events, and who were crowned victors, did not themselves usually ride or drive but employed jockeys and charioteers; but in *Isthmian* 1 for a chariot-race victor, Pindar says that the winner, Herodotus of Thebes, held the reins himself (line 15), as if this was exceptional. In *Isthmian* 4, for a Theban pancratiast, Pindar rather surprisingly says that the victor was of puny appearance (line 50)—perhaps a joke for a fellow Theban. The ordering of the odes, Olympian, Pythian, Nemean, and Isthmian, reflects the order of the games in terms of their importance; within each group of odes those celebrating victories in the chariot race generally come first because it was the event held in greatest esteem. No *Olympian* or *Pythian* ode is for a victor in the pancration, whereas three *Nemeans* and five *Isthmians* are; conversely, eleven *Olympians* and *Pythians*, but only five *Nemeans* and *Isthmians* are for chariot- and horse-race victors. At the major games Pindar focused on the major events.

Outline of an Ode

Pindar's earliest surviving ode is *Pythian* 10 (498 BC). It contains in a relatively straightforward form many of the essential features of a Pindaric ode, features which occur with variations and greater complexity and obscurity in his later odes. A brief analysis of it provides a useful template for application to other odes. He starts with a striking, somewhat cryptic address to Sparta and Thessaly, 'Happy is Lacedaemon, blessed is Thessaly!' He likes a forceful start to his odes (cf. *Olympian* 6.1–3). He mentions Thessaly because that is where the victor he is celebrating came from; he joins it with Sparta probably because of the political situation at the time, when Thessaly allied herself with Sparta against Athens. We are often in the dark over the historical circumstances surrounding Pindar's odes, especially as many of them are of uncertain date. If we knew more of the historical background to them, our appreciation would be enhanced. It would, for example, be rewarding to know whether *Nemean* 7 is apologizing for a harsh treatment of the hero Neoptolemus in one of his other poems, *Paean* 6, or simply presenting the hero in a way befitting a victory ode as opposed to a paean (a poem honouring Apollo);[18] and it is disputed whether the end of the long *Pythian* 4 (lines 267–99) is a plea to King Arcesilaus of Cyrene for the recall from exile of a friend of Pindar's or a compliment to the king for having recalled the friend.[19] He carries on in *Pythian* 10 by saying that the descendants of Heracles rule over both places (lines 2–3), and then (line 3) asks, 'Why do I make this assertion? Do I miss the mark?' On the face of it Pindar seems to be apologizing for having said something out of place, but in fact what we have is a rhetorical question uttered tongue-in-cheek, one of many in the odes (cf. *Pythian* 11.40, *Nemean* 3.26–7); really, he here wants to draw attention to a connection between the victor and the great Heracles, thereby enhancing the victor. In line 5 he mentions how the family who commissioned the ode wants to bring to Hippocleas, the victor, 'the fine voices of men singing in praise' (line 6), indicating that the ode was performed, as most of them seem to have been, by a chorus (cf. *Nemean* 3.4–5). Hippocleas 'tastes' success in the games (line 7). Pindar's bold metaphors are one of the most striking and prevalent features of his poetry, helping to enliven his message and suggest how extraordinary the achievement of victory is. 'Apollo . . . It must be by your devising | that Hippocleas succeeded in this, but it is also by his inborn qualities | that he has walked in the footsteps of his father' (lines 10–11). Here Pindar emphasizes two fundamental beliefs, that human success required the help of the gods and that athletic talent is inborn, not taught (cf. *Olympian* 10.20–1: 'If a man is born for success, another may with a god's help | sharpen his edge and drive him towards prodigious feats of glory'); hence both men and gods feature in Pindar's odes, and wherever possible he lists earlier victories by the victor's ancestors to illustrate the presence of inherited ability (cf. *Olympian* 9.100–1). Hippocleas' father had won twice in the race in armour at the Olympics (two lengths of the stadium, like Hippocleas' own victory) and at the Pythian games. After this mention of the successes of members of the family, Pindar says that he hopes the gods are not jealous of them and that they do not meet with reversals of fortune (lines 20–1). The potential for others, either gods or men, to resent the victorious athlete's success is a

---

[18] See headnote to *Nemean* 7. The *Paeans* are translated in vol. ii of the Loeb edn. of Pindar by W. H. Race.

[19] The headnote to *Pythian* 4 takes the former view.

common motif in Pindar (cf. *Pythian* 7.18–19: 'I am pleased at your recent good fortune, | but grieved that success is repaid with envy'). The very achievement of the victor made him a target for others' ill-will and encouraged the gods to keep a closer eye on him so he did not try to overstep his human limitations; Pindar, too, had to be careful that he did not overstep the mark with his praise and likewise incur hostility.

Nearly all the odes contain at least one sentence where interpretation of the Greek, and how the sentence connects logically with the following one, are disputed. Pindar's style is often cryptic and allusive, and although a performance of an ode must have been a spectacular and enjoyable experience, with dancing and music, how many of the original audience fully grasped all the subtle nuances of the Greek we shall never know; the intellectual abilities of ancient Greek athletes presumably covered as wide a range as that of modern athletes. Pindar composed both for a one-off appreciation at the time of performance and for post-performance perusal of the text (*Olympian* 7 was inscribed in gold in the temple of Athene at Lindos in Rhodes). Lines 21–2 of *Pythian* 10 contain a sentence of four words whose meaning is disputed, either 'May god be unpained at heart' or 'A god's heart may be untouched by pain' or 'May god's heart cause no pain'. The precise connection of thought with both the previous sentence, mentioning the possibility of the gods envying the successes of the victor's family, and the following sentence, saying that a victor is blessed and worthy of a poet's praise, will vary accordingly. Another such cryptic sentence is at *Olympian* 11.10, 'but in the same way it is only through a god's agency | that a man's poetic skill grows to fruition', where it is unclear to what 'in the same way' refers and it has been omitted from this translation. There are many other examples, often at a pivotal place in the ode, linking one part with another and therefore expressed so as to have a double reference.

Then (lines 29–54) comes the mythical section of the ode, here a story about Perseus' journey to the Hyperboreans. Nearly all the odes contain a myth about heroes and heroines of the past who generally have a connection with the victor's homeland. The odes for victors from Aegina, for example, have myths about Aeacus, son of Zeus and the eponymous nymph Aegina, and his descendants. The myths enable Pindar to compare implicitly the victor with heroes of the past and thereby to idealize him. Sometimes Pindar uses the myth as a means of issuing a warning in an indirect way, as when in *Olympian* 1 he tells of how Tantalus, buoyed up by his prosperity, was punished for trying to deceive the gods (lines 36–64); the implication for the victor Hieron, tyrant of Syracuse, is that he must remember his mortal limits. Pindar often tailors the myth to fit in with the victor's circumstances, as when in *Isthmian* 1 he highlights how Castor and Iolaus were the greatest charioteers produced by Sparta and Thebes respectively (lines 16–17), and then runs through their athletics achievements. There were many stories he could have told about these heroes, but *Isthmian* 1 was for a Theban victor in the chariot race who had many other victories to his credit. The Hyperboreans of *Pythian* 10 are a fantastic people of the far north who lived in a blessed condition analogous to that of the victor, but they cannot be reached by ordinary people. So they serve to underline both the special status of the victor and also his limitations. The fact that Perseus, with divine help, once went to them and then returned, highlights another aspect of the victor: his bliss is ephemeral, because for all his success the future is uncertain and he is mortal; similarly in *Olympian* 1, Pelops goes up to Mt. Olympus and then comes back down again to be among mortals. The Hyperboreans have music and garlands and feasting, as the celebrating victor does, but they lack disease, old age, and hardship (not true of the victor). Having spent fifteen lines on the Hyperboreans, Pindar concludes the mythical section with two lines on the myth everyone knew concerning Perseus, how he killed the Gorgon Medusa, brought back her head and turned King Polydectes to stone. It is typical of Pindar to dwell on an invented version of a myth, while touching also on a well-known version. In *Pythian* 12 the myth is also about Perseus. We hear of the death of Medusa and Polydectes' fate, but this time, because the poem is for a winner of a musical event, the pipe-playing competition at the Pythian games, most of the mythical section is about how the sound of the pipes imitates the wailing of Medusa's sisters. At the end of the myth in *Pythian* 10 comes a vivid metaphor to mark how the poem is now moving on to a new theme: 'Ease the oar, quickly drop the anchor from the prow | and drive it into the ground to save us from the rocky reef' (lines 51–2), that is, it is time to end the mythical section. Pindar is a self-conscious poet, regularly inserting himself as a poet into his odes and commenting on the ode's progress. He had a clear conception of what was and what was not appropriate for a victory ode and many times talks about the need for him not to overstep the mark or miss the target or say too much. He had been paid by his patrons to compose victory odes in praise of them, but also had his own poetic agenda, wanting to bring out in his poetry other themes, such as human frailties, the power of the gods, the uncertainty of the future. Sometimes one can detect a tension between these two aspects of his odes, the private and the public voice. In *Pythian* 10 after ending the myth he embarks on a final triad which contains much more direct praise, of the victor, Hippocleas, and of Thorax, head of the powerful Thessalian Aleuadae family which had commissioned the ode. There is also a 'thank-you' to Thorax for his hospitality and beneficence towards Pindar, alluding to the fact that the commissioning of the ode was a financial transaction, and the ode ends with praise of Thessaly's political governance. The perform-ance of *Pythian* 10 would have been part of a public celebration. The last lines of the ode emphasize this aspect, rather as the playing of a victor's national anthem does at a modern games.

The political dimension of Pindar's odes is apparent in many ways. Five of the six odes for the powerful Sicilian tyrants (*Olympians* 1–3, *Pythians* 1–3) contain stories about the punishment of sinners. Pindar wanted to warn these men not to abuse their power. The odes for Aeginetans praise the island's hospitality to visitors and justice (espe-cially its role in helping to defeat the Persians during the Persian Wars). Political disturbance underlies *Olympian* 12 and *Isthmian* 1, exile *Pythians* 4 and 7; *Nemean* 9 praises the military successes of the victor; *Nemean* 11, though mentioning athletics victories, is really a poem honouring a past victor now becoming a high-ranking state official.

One can compare and contrast *Pythian* 10 with what is probably Pindar's latest surviving ode, *Pythian* 8, composed in 446 BC for Aristomenes, a wrestler from Aegina. The two odes share similar themes, but in general he is less direct in the later ode. *Pythian* 8 opens with an invocation to 'Benevolent Concord, daughter of Justice, who makes cities great'; she is thanked for Aristomenes' victory, but Pindar then dwells on how she brings down insolent enemies. Underlying these lines is Aegina's treatment at the hands of Athens a decade earlier when it was forced into the Athenian empire and to pay tribute to Athens. Pindar seems to be taking the opportunity to allude to the possible consequences of Athens' arrogance towards Aegina, and the theme seems to be taken up at the end of the ode when the divinities and heroes associated with Aegina are invoked to protect the island 'on its freeborn voyage' (line 99). There are political resonances here, but nothing overt. Pindar then moves on to the victor's family and tells us that his talent was in the genes: one of his maternal uncles had been an Olympic wrestling victor, and another had won at the Isthmian games. Then follows (lines 39–55) the mythical section of the ode, about the same length as that in *Pythian* 10, but less straightforward: it is about the attacks on Thebes, first the unsuccessful one by the Seven against Thebes, then successfully by their sons the Epigoni, focusing in particular on Amphiareus who perished in the first expedition and his son Alcman, a member of the second. Pindar then, somewhat surprisingly, adds that Adrastus, sole survivor of the first expedition and also a member of the second, alone of the Epigoni lost his son in the second expedition. So beneath the theme of inherited prowess lies also the theme of how intertwined success and loss are, and this reflects the success of Aristomenes in the games and Aegina's loss of freedom. There follows (lines 55–60) one of the most obscure passages in all the odes: 'So spoke Amphiaraus; and I too am glad to throw garlands at Alcman | and to rain hymns on him, because he is my neighbour | and guardian of my wealth, and came to meet me | on my way to the navel-stone of the earth, celebrated in song, | and made use of his prophetic hereditary skills.' It is possible to interpret this quasi-literally: Pindar had a vision of the hero Alcman encountering him (Pindar) as he went to Delphi for the games, in which the hero prophesied to Pindar that Aristomenes would be victorious; and, at a shrine of the hero at Pindar's home city of Thebes, Pindar deposited some of his possessions (perhaps to thank the hero for the prophecy being realized). But the intrusion by the poet of such personal matter seems odd, and no shrines of Alcman at Thebes are known. It seems on balance preferable to interpret the whole episode in a different way, with Pindar speaking metaphorically, imaginatively creating a powerful but fictitious image to link together poet, victory and the theme of inherited prowess, the 'neighbour/guardian' part being a fiction to justify the poet's admiration for the hero, 'on the way to Delphi', preparing us for the move to the next section of the poem which describes Apollo's temple at Delphi and the Pythian games, and Alcman's meeting Pindar and using his inherited prophetic skills illustrating on the heroic level the application of native talent and its relevance to the poet's theme. If this interpretation is on the right lines, Pindar is resuming the covert type of composition we observed at the start of the poem. However, the use of imaginative and metaphorical fictions in this way, especially as a means to pass from one section of a poem to another, is not new. In *Pythian* 11, at the end of the myth, he pretends he has gone off course either on the road or at sea: he must get back on course by quitting the myth and returning to praise of the victor and his family (lines 38 ff.). Perhaps more akin to our passage is *Pythian* 3.77–9, where Pindar says he would have come as a saviour to Hieron (who was in ill-health) but cannot: 'But I wish to pray to the Mother, the revered goddess, | to whom, with Pan, girls often sing before my door at night.' Though sometimes interpreted literally (Pindar having a shrine to Pan and the Mother Goddess by his house), it seems better to see it again as an imaginative and metaphorical fiction designed to justify why the poet cannot come to Hieron's aid. In *Pythian* 8, after the address to Apollo and the customary mention of the victor's father and family, there is a brief list of previous victories by Aristomenes (a victory list, if available, is a standard ingredient of the odes), and then a most vivid last section of the poem (lines 81–97) highlighting on the one hand the glory and splendour of victory, but also the short-livedness and shame of defeat. Here Pindar puts the achievement of victory into a larger context: even someone who has achieved something great is still only a mortal human being for whom joys do not last long. 'What is man? What is he not?' (line 95), that is, what is the difference between the successful and those who fail, given that even the successful are destined to die. 'He is the dream of a shadow' (line 95), that is, insignificant in the scheme of things. 'Yet when Zeus-sent brightness comes | a brilliant light shines upon mankind and their life is serene' (lines 96–7). The idea that the glory associated with success requires the help of the gods is common in Pindar. All the themes of this last section are found in abundance elsewhere in the odes; nowhere are they more forcefully expressed. This exemplifies Pindar's greatest achievement. His subject matter is mundane: athletics success, man's relationship to gods and heroes, myths, moralizing; the last four common in most ancient Greek literature. But the way he expresses himself on these topics can be extraordinary.

Pindar's Influence

'What is rare is valuable; water is very cheap, though best, as Pindar says.' Plato here[20] alludes to the beginning of *Olympian* 1. He admired Pindar, especially for his moral and religious outlook, and quotes from him a number of times; many other Classical authors also refer to him.[21] The victory ode did not die out after Pindar and Bacchylides: Euripides wrote one celebrating the successes in the chariot race of the maverick Athenian general Alcibiades in the late fifth century, and fragments of two by Callimachus in the third century survive. But Callimachus' work was intended to be read, not performed; what survived of Pindar was his literary style. Particularly influential was the allusive nature of his poetry, the ode form (in Greek, repeated groups of lines of unequal length and rhythm), and his bold images and metaphors. Pindar often compares (and contrasts) his poetry to architecture (memorably at the beginning of *Olympian* 6 and *Nemean* 5). Virgil, at the start of his Third *Georgic* uses this motif in a section of the poem praising Octavian; its Pindaric pedigree adds grandeur to the praise. Horace, like Pindar, composed four books of odes but in general they have more in common with Greek lyric poetry by authors other than Pindar. Horace tells us why: 'Whoever strives to rival Pindar, Iulus, is relying on wings joined with wax by the skill of Daedalus and is destined to give his name to the glassy sea. Like a stream running down from a mountain, a stream which the rains have swollen over its familiar banks, Pindar boils and rushes without measure with unrestrained voice.'[22] Pindar's odes were composed to be part of a lively outdoor victory celebration (*kōmos*); some aspects of them were regarded as inappropriate to a purely literary context.

After the English Renaissance, with the rebirth of interest in Classical literature, Ben Jonson and Abraham Cowley in the seventeenth century wrote odes reminiscent of Pindar's. The irregularity

---

[20] *Euthydemus* 304b. Some material in this section comes from S. Instone, *Pindar: Selected Odes* (Warminster, 1996), 22–9, and J. T. Hamilton, *Soliciting Darkness: Pindar, Obscurity and the Classical Tradition* (Cambridge, Mass., and London, 2003).

[21] See the 'Index Fontium' (List of Sources), pp. 207–24 at the back of vol. ii of the Teubner edition of Pindar, ed. H. Maehler (Leipzig, 1989). The list includes Aristophanes, Callimachus, Cicero, Herodotus, Horace, Isocrates, Lucian, Menander, Pausanias, Plautus, and Plutarch. Thucydides, too, was probably familiar with Pindar's work: see Hornblower, *Thucydides and Pindar*.

[22] Horace, *Odes* 4.1–8.

of the length and rhythm of Pindar's lines, and Pindar's wealth of vivid images, attracted them. Cowley, like Horace, was aware of the dangers of imitating too closely: 'If a man should undertake to translate Pindar word for word, it would be thought that one Mad man had translated another.'[23] After Cowley, Dryden wrote a number of odes with a Pindaric flavour. 'A Song for St Cecelia's Day' and 'Alexander's Feast' were written for musical performance, and in this respect they revived an essential feature of Pindar's odes that had been ignored by Jonson and Cowley. In the eighteenth century Thomas Gray's *Progress of Poesy: a Pindaric Ode* ('Awake, Aeolian lyre, awake . . .') is strongly influenced by Pindaric metaphors. But again, like Cowley, Gray realizes that Pindar is inimitable: 'Oh! lyre divine, what daring spirit | Wakes thee now? Though he inherit | Nor the pride nor ample pinion, | That the Theban eagle bear | Sailing with supreme dominion | Through the azure deep of air . . .'. In Germany, Goethe (1749–1832) and Hölderlin (1770–1843) were indebted to Pindar in their lyrics. Goethe admired Pindar's obscurity and difficulty. Hölderlin even produced interpretative translations of some of the surviving fragments of Pindaric poetry. Pindar's victory odes provided, and continue to provide, an aesthetic and intellectual challenge. We today can also value them for what they tell us about ancient Greek athletics, and for the rightful importance they attach to sport, competition, and physical exercise.

[23] Preface to his *Pindarique Odes*, published in 1656.

TRANSLATOR'S NOTE

Pindar is a notoriously hard nut for translators to crack. The odes' idiom and their social context are so far removed from modern experience that a translation tends to lurch towards one of two extremes: overdependence on the Greek and so requiring hatfuls of explanatory notes, or excessive 'interpretation', thereby losing some of the immediacy of Pindar's unique style. Both run the risk of baffling the reader. There is no easy fix; all one can do is to choose roughly where on this spectrum one's version ideally lies, and hope for the reader's cooperation. Luckily, Pindar's poetic virtues are so strong that whatever one does to him one cannot prevent his genius breaking through—especially in the odes' central glorious myth-telling sections.

In accordance with Oxford World's Classics policy, this translation keeps as close as it can to the Greek without sacrificing sense. For example, Pindar's sometimes violent leaps of imagery are where possible left to speak for themselves. I have, however, occasionally expanded his (wilfully?) compressed sentence-structure in the interests of clarity and ease of reading.

Pindar wrote his odes in complex metrical schemes, often in repeated 'triads' in which two identically metrical groups of verses ('strophe' and 'antistrophe') are followed by a third ('epode') in a related but different metre; or sometimes in a monostrophic structure (all the groups of verses in the same metre). Since it is impossible to retain these metres in an English version, it makes little sense to divide up the translation of each ode in the manner of the original Greek text. In this translation breaks within an ode follow breaks in sense, in the hope that it will become clear when Pindar is moving on to a new theme.

Three scholars have helped me enormously in this enterprise, guiding me through Pindar's real or imagined obscurities and saving me from errors of interpretation: Stephen Instone (who has written the Introduction and Notes), Peter Jones, and Malcolm Willcock (who died unexpectedly just as the translation was completed). Any infelicities which remain are entirely mine.

The translation is based on the eighth Teubner edition of Pindar's epinicians by B. Snell and H. Maehler (Leipzig, 1987), with one or two variations. Marginal line numbers and references to line numbers refer to the original Greek text.

SELECT BIBLIOGRAPHY

Editions and Commentaries

There is an excellent two-volume edition of Pindar (with Greek text, notes, and translation) by W. H. Race in the Loeb Classical Library series (Cambridge, Mass., and London, 1997). Commentaries on individual odes, or selections of odes, are mentioned below.

General

C. M. Bowra, *Pindar* (Oxford, 1964).

D. S. Carne-Ross, *Pindar* (New Haven and London, 1985).

S. Hornblower and C. Morgan (eds.), *Pindar's Poetry, Patrons, and Festivals: From Archaic Greece to the Roman Empire* (Oxford, 2007).

W. H. Race, *Pindar* (Boston, 1986).

The Historical Background

S. Hornblower, *Thucydides and Pindar* (Oxford, 2004).

The Religious Background

B. Currie, *Pindar and the Cult of Heroes* (Oxford, 2005).

Pythian Odes

R. W. B. Burton, *Pindar's Pythian Odes: Essays in Interpretation* (Oxford, 1962).

Aeginetan Odes

A. Pippin Burnett, *Pindar's Songs for Young Athletes of Aigina* (Oxford, 2005).

Pindar's Influence

J. T. Hamilton, *Soliciting Darkness: Pindar, Obscurity and the Classical Tradition* (Cambridge, Mass., and London, 2003).

Individual Odes

Olympian 1

S. Instone, *Pindar: Selected Odes* (Warminster, 1996), 89–116.

Olympian 2

M. M. Willcock, *Pindar: Victory Odes* (Cambridge, 1995), 133–74.

Olympian 3

D. S. Carne-Ross, *Pindar* (New Haven and London, 1985), 50–9.

E. Krummen, *Pyrsos Hymnon: Festliche Gegenwart und Mythisch-Rituelle Tradition bei Pindar* (Berlin and New York, 1990), 217–66.

Olympians 4 and 5

W. Mader, *Die Psaumis-Oden Pindars (O. 4 & O. 5): ein Kommentar* (Innsbruck, 1990).

Olympian 6

G. Kirkwood, *Selections from Pindar* (Chico, Calif., 1982), 79–96.

Olympian 7

M. M. Willcock, *Pindar: Victory Odes* (Cambridge, 1995), 109–33.

Olympian 8

A. Pippin Burnett, *Pindar's Songs for Young Athletes of Aigina* (Oxford, 2005), 203–19.

Olympian 9

D. E. Gerber, *A Commentary on Pindar Olympian Nine* (Stuttgart, 2002).

Olympian 10

W. H. Race, *Pindar* (Boston, 1986), 116–20.

Olympian 11

M. M. Willcock, *Pindar: Victory Odes* (Cambridge, 1995), 55–60.

Olympian 12

M. Silk, in S. Hornblower and C. Morgan (eds.), *Pindar's Poetry, Patrons, and Festivals: From Archaic Greece to the Roman Empire* (Oxford, 2007).

Olympian 13

C. Morgan, in S. Hornblower and C. Morgan (eds.), *Pindar's Poetry, Patrons, and Festivals: From Archaic Greece to the Roman Empire* (Oxford, 2007).

Olympian 14

D. S. Carne-Ross, *Pindar* (New Haven and London, 1985), 59–66.

Pythian 1

D. S. Carne-Ross, *Pindar* (New Haven and London, 1985), 101–10.

Pythian 2

B. Currie, *Pindar and the Cult of Heroes* (Oxford, 2005), 258–95.

H. Lloyd-Jones, 'Modern Interpretation of Pindar', *Journal of Hellenic Studies*, 93 (1973), 117–25.

Pythian 3

B. Currie, *Pindar and the Cult of Heroes* (Oxford, 2005), 344–405.

Pythians 4 and 5

B. K. Braswell, *A Commentary on the Fourth Pythian Ode of Pindar* (Berlin and New York, 1988).

S. Hornblower, *Thucydides and Pindar* (Oxford, 2004), 107–13 (on the colonization of Cyrene).

E. Krummen, *Pyrsos Hymnon: Festliche Gegenwart und Mythisch-Rituelle Tradition bei Pindar* (Berlin and New York, 1990), 98–151 (on *P.* 5).

C. Segal, *Pindar's Mythmaking: The Fourth Pythian Ode* (Princeton, 1986).

Pythian 6

W. H. Race, *Pindar* (Boston, 1986), 85–91.

Pythian 7

R. W. B. Burton, *Pindar's Pythian Odes: Essays in Interpretation* (Oxford, 1962), 32–5.

Pythian 8

M. Lefkowitz, 'Pindar's Pythian 8', *Classical Journal*, 72 (1977), 209–21.

I. L. Pfeijffer, *Three Aeginetan Odes of Pindar* (Leiden, 1999), 423–602.

A. Pippin Burnett, *Pindar's Songs for Young Athletes of Aigina* (Oxford, 2005), 220–38.

Pythian 9

S. Instone, *Pindar: Selected Odes* (Warminster, 1996), 117–42.

Pythian 10

A. Köhnken, *Die Funktion des Mythos bei Pindar* (Berlin and New York, 1971), 154–87.

Pythian 11

S. Instone, 'Pythian 11: Did Pindar Err?', *Classical Quarterly*, 36 (1986), 86–94.

D. C. Young, *Three Odes of Pindar*, *Mnemosyne*, Suppl. 9 (1968), 1–26.

Pythian 12

A. Köhnken, 'Perseus' Kampf und Athenes Erfindung (Bemerkungen zu Pindar, Pythien 12)', *Hermes*, 104 (1976), 257–65.

Nemean 1

B. K. Braswell, *A Commentary on Pindar Nemean One* (Fribourg, 1992).

Nemean 2

S. Instone, *Pindar: Selected Odes* (Warminster, 1986), 143–51.

Nemean 3

S. Instone, *Pindar: Selected Odes* (Warminster, 1996), 152–69.
I. L. Pfeijffer, *Three Aeginetan Odes of Pindar* (Leiden, 1999), 195–421.
A. Pippin Burnett, *Pindar's Songs for Young Athletes of Aigina* (Oxford, 2005), 136–52.

Nemean 4

A. Pippin Burnett, *Pindar's Songs for Young Athletes of Aigina* (Oxford, 2005), 119–35.
M. M. Willcock, *Pindar: Victory Odes* (Cambridge, 1995), 91–109.

Nemean 5

I. L. Pfeijffer, *Three Aeginetan Odes of Pindar* (Leiden, 1999), 57–193.
A. Pippin Burnett, *Pindar's Songs for Young Athletes of Aigina* (Oxford, 2005), 57-76.

Nemean 6

C. Carey, 'Prosopographica Pindarica', *Classical Quarterly*, 39 (1989), 6–9.
A. Pippin Burnett, *Pindar's Songs for Young Athletes of Aigina* (Oxford, 2005), 153–63.

Nemean 7

H. Lloyd-Jones, 'Modern Interpretation of Pindar: The Second Pythian and Seventh Nemean Odes', *Journal of Hellenic Studies*, 93 (1973), 127–37.
A. Pippin Burnett, *Pindar's Songs for Young Athletes of Aigina* (Oxford, 2005), 179–202.
R. Rutherford, *Pindar's Paeans* (Oxford, 2001), 321–3.

Nemean 8

A. Pippin Burnett, *Pindar's Songs for Young Athletes of Aigina* (Oxford, 2005), 164–78.

Nemean 9

B. K. Braswell, *A Commentary on Pindar Nemean Nine* (Berlin and New York, 1998).

Nemean 10

W. B. Henry, *Pindar's Nemeans: A Selection* (Munich and Leipzig, 2005), 91–118.

D. S. Carne-Ross, *Pindar* (New Haven and London, 1985), 79–90.

Nemean 11

M. Lefkowitz, 'Pindar's Nemean XI', *Journal of Hellenic Studies*, 19 (1979), 49–56.

Isthmian 1

E. L. Bundy, *Studia Pindarica*, 2 (Berkeley and Los Angeles, 1986), 35–92.

S. Instone, *Pindar: Selected Odes* (Warminster, 1986), 170–88.

Isthmian 2

W. H. Race, *Pindar* (Boston, 1986), 85–91.

Isthmians 3 and 4

E. Krummen, *Pyrsos Hymnon: Festliche Gegenwart und Mythisch-Rituelle Tradition bei Pindar* (Berlin and New York, 1990), 33–97 (on *I.* 4).

M. M. Willcock, *Pindar: Victory Odes* (Cambridge, 1995), 69–91.

Isthmian 5

A. Pippin Burnett, *Pindar's Songs for Young Athletes of Aigina* (Oxford, 2005), 89–101.

Isthmian 6

A. Pippin Burnett, *Pindar's Songs for Young Athletes of Aigina* (Oxford, 2005), 77–88.

Isthmian 7

B. Currie, Pindar and the Cult of Heroes (Oxford, 2005), 205–25.

M. M. Willcock, *Pindar: Victory Odes* (Cambridge, 1995), 60–9.

Isthmian 8

D. S. Carne-Ross, *Pindar* (New Haven and New York, 1985), 121–30.

Further Reading in Oxford World's Classics

John Dryden, *The Major Works*, ed. Keith Walker.

Greek Lyric Poetry, trans. M. L. West.

The Homeric Hymns, trans. Michael Crudden.

CHRONOLOGY

All dates are BC.

776   Traditional foundation date of Olympic games (held every four years).

c.750–725   *Iliad* and *Odyssey* composed.

586 or 582   Traditional foundation date of Pythian games (held every four years).

582   Traditional foundation date of Isthmian games (held every two years).

573   Traditional foundation date of Nemean games (held every two years).

525/4   Aeschylus born.

518   Pindar born.

490s   New temple of Aphaea built on Aegina.

498   Pindar's earliest surviving ode, *Pythian* 10.

496/5   Sophocles born.

490   Persian Wars: Battle of Marathon.

490–480   Herodotus born.

480s   Euripides born.

480–479   Persian Wars: Battles of Salamis and Plataea.

470s   Pindar's odes for the Sicilian tyrants: *Olympians* 1–3, *Pythians* 1–3.

462   Pindar's odes for Arcesilas, king of Cyrene: *Pythians* 4 and 5.

460–455   Thucydides born.

458–457   Aegina forced into the Athenian empire.

446   Pindar's latest surviving ode, *Pythian* 8.

THE ODES

OLYMPIANS

OLYMPIAN 1

For Hieron of Syracuse, winner of the single-horse race

Water is best,*
while gold gleams like blazing fire in the night,
brightest amid a rich man's wealth;
but, my heart, if it is of games that you wish to sing,
look no further than the sun: as there is no star
that shines with more warmth by day from a clear sky,
so we can speak of no greater contest than Olympia.*
From here come fame-giving hymns,
which wrap themselves around the minds of poets*
who have come to the rich and blessed hearth of Hieron
to sing aloud of the son of Cronus.*   10
Hieron holds the sceptre of justice in sheep-rich Sicily,
where he chooses for himself the finest fruits
of every kind of excellence.
His glory gleams in the best of poetry and music,
of the kind that we men often compose in play
at his hospitable table.

Come then, take down the Dorian* lyre from its peg,
if the splendour of Olympian Pisa* and of Pherenicus*
has caused the sweetest thoughts to steal into your mind,
as it sped along unwhipped in the race beside Alpheus,*   20
and brought its master into victory's embrace—
Hieron, Syracuse's horse-delighting king.
His fame shines out over the land
of fine men* founded by Lydian Pelops,*
he whom Poseidon the mighty Earth-holder desired
after Clotho* had lifted him from the purifying cauldron,*
fitted with a shoulder of gleaming ivory.

There are indeed many wonders,
and it may be that in men's talk

stories are embroidered beyond the truth,
and so deceive us with their elaborate lies,
since the beguiling charm of words,
the source of all sweet pleasures for men,   30
adds lustre and veracity to the unbelievable.
The days to come will be the wisest judge of that,
but it is proper that a man should speak well of the gods;
thus he is less likely to incur blame.

Son of Tantalus, the tale I shall tell about you
runs counter to that told by former poets.
When your father invited the gods
to that well-ordered banquet in his beloved Sipylus,*
reciprocating the hospitality he had enjoyed,
then it was that the God of the Glorious Trident,*   40
his heart overpowered by desire,
seized you and carried you off in a golden chariot
to the lofty palace of widely honoured Zeus,
where in later time Ganymede* also came,
to perform the same service, but for Zeus.
When you had disappeared from sight,
and, despite their frequent searches,
no one could bring you back to your mother,
immediately an ill-intentioned neighbour
secretly spread the tale abroad
that the guests had taken a knife and dismembered you,
and had thrown your limbs into water
as it boiled fiercely over the fire;   50
and then at table, during the final course,
they shared out your flesh and ate it.
As for me, I cannot call any of the blessed gods a cannibal.
I stand aside;
the slanderous seldom win themselves profit.

If ever the watchers on Olympus* gave a mortal honour,
that man indeed was Tantalus.*
But no good came of it, for he could not digest his great prosperity,
and by his excesses brought overwhelming ruin on himself:
the Father poised a huge stone above him,
and in his constant struggle to thrust it from his head

he now wanders far from happiness.
This is the life of everlasting weariness he lives,
one labour following after another,   60
because for his feast he stole from the gods
the nectar and ambrosia they gave to make him immortal
and served it to his drinking companions.
If a man hopes his deeds will escape the gods' notice
he is mistaken.

So the immortals sent his son back to him,
to be a mortal again in the short-lived company of men.
And about the time of his handsome youthful bloom,
when downy hair began to cover his darkening jaw,
he turned his thoughts to an offer of marriage
that was offered to all: to win at Pisa
the famous Hippodameia* from her father Oenomaus.   70

Alone, at night, he went down to the grey sea's shore
and called out to the deep-roaring Lord of the Trident;*
and the god was there, close by him.
Pelops said to him:
'If the delightful gifts of Cypris* can give rise to gratitude,
then come, shackle the bronze spear of Oenomaus,
send me on the swiftest of chariots to Elis,*
and bring me the power to be victorious.
Thirteen suitors has Oenomaus killed,
and in this way delays the marriage of his daughter.   80
Cowards do not seek out great risks;
men must die, so why should anyone crouch in darkness,
aimlessly nursing an undistinguished old age,
without a share in glorious deeds?
This contest is meant for me; now give me the success I desire.'

So he spoke, and his pleas were not in vain.
The god gave him honour,
and a golden chariot with tireless winged horses.
So he defeated Oenomaus, and won the maiden to share his bed,
and fathered six sons, leaders of the people,
all of them thirsting to do great deeds.
And now he luxuriates in splendid blood-offerings*   90

as he reclines beside the ford of Alpheus.
His tomb beside his altar is well tended,
thronged about by many a stranger.

The fame which stems from Pelops' games at Olympia
is visible from afar—the games where
the contest is for fleetness of foot
and daring deeds of strength pushed to the limit.
For the rest of his days the victor enjoys honey-sweet tranquillity,
as far, that is, as the games can provide it;
the highest good for every mortal
is indeed that which comes to him day by day.   100

My task is to crown such a man as this
with the horseman's song, in Aeolian melody.*
I am certain that there is no host today
more acquainted with glorious deeds
or more established in his power,
whom my craft can adorn with fame-giving intricacies of song.
Some god, Hieron, watches over your ambitions,
making this his concern. If he does not desert you
I hope to find an even more inviting path of poetry
to help me celebrate your victory in the swift chariot,   110
when I visit the sunlit hill of Cronus.*

For me, the Muse keeps a mighty defensive weapon.
Other men attain greatness in different ways;
the highest peaks are occupied by kings,
so do not look to climb further.
May you walk on high in this reign of yours,
and may I always be the victors' companion,
pre-eminent by my poetry throughout all Hellas.

OLYMPIAN 2

For Theron of Acragas, winner of the chariot race

My hymns, commanders of the lyre,
which god, which hero—which man* shall we celebrate?
Zeus is indeed lord of Pisa, and Heracles
founded the Olympic games as the first-fruits of war;
but the man we must proclaim is Theron,
for his victory with the four-horsed chariot.
He is just in his regard for strangers,
a strong tower of defence for Acragas,
the crowning glory of a famous family line,
a man who guides his city on a straight path.
His forebears laboured hard* in their hearts
and so won a holy habitation beside the river.
They were the envy of Sicily,   10
and as time sped them on its destined road
it added wealth and popular favour to crown their inborn talents.

Son of Cronus and Rhea,*
you who rule over your home on Olympus,
and over this greatest of games and Alpheus' stream;
be warmed by my songs and in your kindness
preserve their native land for generations to come.

But when some deed has been done, right or wrong,*
not even Time the father of all things can undo its outcome;
yet with the help of good fortune men may forget it.
Grief dies when confronted by noble joys,
and its enduring bitterness is beaten down   20
when fortune sent from a god
lifts a man to prosperity's heights.

This saying fits the royal-throned daughters of Cadmus,*
whose sufferings were great;
yet even so, heavy sorrow sinks back
in the face of mightier blessings.
Long-haired Semele died amid the roar of thunder,

but she lives on among the Olympian gods,
loved for all time by Pallas and Father Zeus,
and especially loved by her ivy-wearing son.
Ino, too, men say, was granted an immortal's life   30
for all time in the depths, along with Nereus'* sea-nymph
    daughters.

But for mortals death's final point has not been fixed,
nor even when we shall peacefully conclude our day,
child of the sun, in lasting good fortune.
Streams of pleasure and pain flood over men at different times;
and so it is that Fate, which controls the benevolent destiny
that this family has enjoyed, can bring some suffering
even into their heaven-sent prosperity,
which in time to come may be reversed—
from the time when Laius' son* met his father
and, as had been foretold, killed him,
so fulfilling the oracle delivered long before at Pytho.   40
The sharp-eyed Fury saw this act,
and slew his warlike sons, who died at each other's hands.
When Polynices fell he left behind his son Thersandrus,
who won honour both in young men's contests
and in the battles of war—a young shoot from Adrastus'
    stock,
destined to be an avenger of his house.

It is fitting that the son of Aenesidamus,*
whose roots are traced back to that seed,
should enjoy the praise of songs and of the lyre,
for at Olympia he received the prize himself,
while at Pytho and the Isthmus the Graces who favour both   50
awarded the crown in the twelve-lap four-horse chariot race
equally to his brother.*

For a man who competes in the games
victory brings relief from dark thoughts.
Truly wealth, adorned with many noble qualities,
offers a man the chance to achieve all manner of things,
and prompts in him a desire for high ambition,
which is a far-shining star, the surest light there is for men.

If a man possesses wealth, and knows the future—*
that the defenceless spirits of those who die here are quickly
    punished,
and that for crimes committed here in Zeus' kingdom
there is a judge below the earth who declares sentence of
    harsh necessity.   60
But for good men the nights and sunny days
are in perpetual equal balance;* they enjoy a life with less toil,
not troubling the earth or sea's waters with their hands' strength
in order to produce a meagre livelihood.
Those who in life took pleasure in keeping oaths
pass their time without tears in the company of the
    revered gods,
while the wicked endure a punishment too dreadful to behold.
But those with the courage to have lived three times in
    either place,
keeping their hearts entirely free from wrongdoing,
travel the road of Zeus to the tower of Cronus,   70
where breezes of Ocean blow round the island of the blessed.*
There flowers of gold shine like flame,
some on bright trees on the land, some nourished by the sea;
with these they weave bracelets for their arms and crowns for
    their heads,
according to the equitable judgements of Rhadamanthys,*
whom at all times the great father, husband of Rhea,
she who occupies the highest throne, seats beside himself.

Peleus and Cadmus are counted among their company,
and Achilles, brought there by his mother   80
when by her prayers she had won over the heart of Zeus.
Achilles it was who felled Hector, Troy's indomitable
    mighty pillar,
and who brought Cycnus* to death,
and the Ethiopian, son of the dawn.*

I have many swift arrows in the quiver under my arm.
They speak to those who understand,
but for the most part they require interpreters.
Wise is the man who knows much by nature,
while those who have acquired their knowledge

chatter in pointless confusion, just like
a pair of crows against the divine bird of Zeus.*

Come, my heart, aim your bow at the mark!
Who are we now to strike, as we shoot fame's arrows   90
with gentle intent? I bend my bow at Acragas,
proclaiming on oath and with true understanding
that no city in a hundred years has given birth to a man
more generous in spirit to his friends
or more open-handed than Theron.
But praise can soon turn out to be excessive
if it is not attended by impartiality,
but comes from the mouths of the disaffected,
who seek with idle chatter to obscure good men's noble deeds.
As surely as grains of sand are beyond counting,
who could say how many acts of kindness
this man has performed for other men?   100

OLYMPIAN 3

For Theron of Acragas, winner of the chariot race

To please the hospitable sons of Tyndareus
and Helen of the beautiful hair,
and to honour famous Acragas is my prayer,
as I begin a hymn to Theron for his Olympic victory;
this is the finest reward
for horses with never-wearying hoofs.*
This is why, I believe, the Muse stood beside me
as I composed in a brilliant new way
to fit my voice of glorious celebration to the Dorian measure;*
since the victory wreaths woven in his hair
exact payment from me of this god-inspired debt:
to combine in due harmony the many-voiced lyre, the cry of
   pipes,
and the placement of words in honour of Aenesidamus' son.*

Pisa too instructs me to speak out: 10
for from there come god-given songs to men,
whenever the unswerving Hellene judge, an Elean of Aetolian
   stock,*
fulfilling Heracles' ancient orders, sets above a man's brow
the glory of the grey-green olive in his hair,
which once Amphitryon's son* brought from Istrus'*
   shadowed springs
to be the supreme memorial of contests at Olympia.

Heracles had by his eloquence won over
the Hyperborean people,* Apollo's servants.
With honourable intent he begged from them
for the all-welcoming grove of Zeus
a tree to furnish shade for all,
and to be a crown for deeds of prowess.
For by now altars had been dedicated to his father,*
and the gold-charioted moon at mid-month evening
had shone her eye full upon him.   20
He had laid down the great games' holy principle of judgement,

and had established the four-year cycle for his festival,
to be held beside the sacred banks of Alpheus;
but the land of Pelops grew no lovely trees
in the dales of the son of Cronus.
Without their protection this enclosure seemed to him
to be at the mercy of the sun's burning rays.

It was then his spirit moved him to go to the land of Istrus.
There Leto's daughter,* driver of horses, had welcomed him
from Arcadia's mountain ridges and its secret twisting places,
when in obedience to Eurystheus'* commands
and under duress from his father
he was ordered to capture the doe with golden horns
which once the nymph Taygeta had dedicated
to be a sacred offering to Orthosia.   30
In his pursuit of her he came to see the land
that lies beyond the blasts of the icy North Wind.
There he stood and marvelled at the trees,
and a sweet desire seized him to plant some
around the point in the twelve-lap course where horses turn.
And so today he gladly attends this his festival
with the godlike twins, sons of deep-girdled Leto.

Departing for Olympus he instructed them
to take charge of the admired games,
where men compete in prowess and swift chariots are driven.
And so, I believe, my spirit urges me to tell Theron
and the Emmenidae* that glory has come to them
through the gift of the sons of Tyndareus, expert horsemen,
because of all mortals they honour them
with the most numerous hospitable feasts,   40
preserving by their pious intention the rites of the
    blessed gods.

If water is best,* and gold the most revered of all possessions,
now Theron in his turn, by his deeds of merit,
has travelled from his home to the world's limits
and lays hold of the pillars of Heracles.
Further than this neither simpletons nor wise should go.
I shall not venture there; I should be a fool to try.

OLYMPIAN 4

For Psaumis of Camarina, winner of the chariot race (?)

Supreme charioteer of the tireless-footed thunder,
Zeus;* you I invoke because your Seasons,
circling to the sound of the many-voiced lyre,
have sent me to be a witness at the greatest games.
When friends achieve success,
men forthwith feel joy at the welcome news.

Come, son of Cronus, you who reign over Aetna,
windswept cap of powerful hundred-headed Typhos'* prison,
receive this Olympic victor and, to please the Graces,
welcome this revelling procession, a longest-shining light   10
on noble deeds of mighty strength.
It comes* in honour of the chariot of Psaumis,
who was crowned at Pisa with a garland of olive,
and makes haste to bring glory to Camarina.
May the god listen kindly to his prayers in time to come,
for I praise him as a diligent rearer of horses,
a man who delights in offering hospitality to all,
and whose candid manner inclines him
towards Concord,* the friend of cities.

I shall not stain my tale with a lie;
the true test of men is endurance to the end.
This it was that saved the son of Clymenus*
from losing face among the women of Lemnos.   20
He had won the race in bronze armour,
and going up to Hypsipyle to receive his crown, said:
'You have seen my speed; my hands and heart are equally
    strong.
Often even young men produce grey hairs
before the time they are expected to appear.'

OLYMPIAN 5

For Psaumis of Camarina, winner of the mule race

Camarina, daughter of Oceanus,* accept with a joyful heart
this sweet offering, a supreme reward
for high deeds of prowess and crowns won at Olympia:
a gift of Psaumis and his tireless-footed* mules.
He has glorified your city, nurse of people,
and has honoured the six double-altars*
at the god's greatest festival with ox sacrifices
and, in the strenuous five-day games,
with races of chariots, mules, and the single horse.
Victorious, he has made you an offering of lavish glory,
spreading abroad the fame of his father Acron
and of his newly founded city.

O Pallas,* protector of cities, he has come   10
from the beautiful dwellings of Pelops and Oenomaus,*
and he sings in praise of your sacred grove
and Oanos your river and its neighbouring lake,
and the holy channels through which the Hipparis*
brings water to your people.
Swiftly he constructs a lofty grove of well-built houses*
and leads your townspeople here from despair into the light.

Always, when men strive for excellence,
toil and expense struggle towards an accomplishment
in which risk lies concealed.
But the successful are judged to be wise,
even by their fellow citizens.

O saviour Zeus, high above us in the clouds,
inhabitant of the hill of Cronus,
you who honour broad-flowing Alpheus and Ida's holy cave,*
to you I come as suppliant, accompanied by Lydian pipes,*
to beg you to adorn this city with a noble race of men,
and to ask that you, Olympic victor,   20
delighting in the horses of Poseidon,

may bring your old age to a serene end
with your sons, Psaumis, by your side.
If a man waters a healthy prosperity
and is content with a sufficiency of possessions,
and adds to this good repute,
he should not strive to become a god.

OLYMPIAN 6

For Hagesias of Syracuse, winner of the mule race

Golden are the pillars we shall set beneath the chamber's
    well-made porch,
as if we were building a marvellous palace.
When a work is begun its outward face must be made to
    gleam afar;
and if a man should be victorious at Olympia,
and is a steward of the prophetic altar of Zeus* at Pisa,
and moreover a joint founder* of famous Syracuse—
how could such a man escape a celebratory hymn,
if he chances to live among townsmen
who do not stint their tribute of pleasing songs?

Let Sostratus' son* know that this is the sandal
to which the heavenly powers have fitted his foot.
Success without labour is not honoured among men,
either on land or in hollow ships;   10
but if noble deeds are accomplished through toil
many people remember them.
Men are ready to praise you, Hagesias,
as once Adrastus justly spoke out in praise of Amphiaraus,*
son of Oecles, when the earth swallowed him and his
    shining horses.
Later, when the corpses had been burnt on their seven pyres,
Talaus' son spoke in Thebes as follows:
'I grieve for the loss of my army's eye,
a man skilled as a seer and also as a spear-fighter.'

This too can be said of the Syracusan master of this revel.
I am not disputatious, nor over-eager for victory,
but I will swear a great oath and testify   20
that this is true, and the sweet-voiced Muses will bear me out.
Come, Phintis,* quickly yoke me the strong mules,
that I may drive my chariot on an open road
and arrive at this family's true origin. These mules,
more than others, know how to take the lead on this road,

for they have won crowns at Olympia.
We must therefore throw wide the gates of song for them
and come today in good time to Pitane,*
beside the waters of Eurotas.*

She it was, men say, who coupled with Cronus' son Poseidon
and bore a daughter, Euadne of the violet-coloured hair.   30
She concealed the fruit of her unwedded labour
by the folds of her dress, and in her birth-month
despatched her maids to Aepytus, the hero son of Eilatus,*
with orders to deliver the child into his keeping.
He was king of the Arcadians of Phaesane,
and had his allotted home beside the Alpheus.
Here Euadne was raised, and here she gave herself to Apollo
and first tasted the delights of Aphrodite.
But she could not hide the god's seed from Aepytus for ever;
with painful self-control he thrust down in his heart
the anger he could not speak of, and went to Pytho
to consult the oracle concerning his intolerable grief.

Meanwhile she had laid aside her purple belt and silver jug,   40
and in a dark copse began the birth of a son with the spirit
    of a god.
To help her, the golden-haired god* sent the Fates
and Eleithyia, giver of gentle counsel.
Without delay, in joyful birth-pangs
Iamus issued from her womb into the light.
In her distress she left him there on the ground,
but by the gods' designs two grey-eyed snakes nurtured him,
feeding him on the blameless venom of bees.*

When the king had driven back from rocky Pytho
he questioned everyone in the house about the boy Euadne
    had borne,
because, he said, his father was Phoebus,
and he would surpass all mortals as a seer for mankind,   50
and his posterity would never fail. This much he revealed;
but they claimed that though the boy was five days old
they had neither seen nor heard of him.
And in truth he had been hidden on a bed of rushes

under a great bush, his tender body suffused
with the gold and purple radiance of violets;
and this is why his mother had declared that for all time
he would be known by this immortal name.*

When in time he plucked the fruit of lovely gold-crowned
   youth,
he waded midstream into the Alpheus
and called on Poseidon the wide ruler, his grandfather,
and on the bow-handler, guardian of god-built Delos.
Under the open night sky he asked for himself
an office in which he could minister to his people.   60
Clear came his father's voice in answer, saying:
'Arise, my son, and accompany my voice
to a land which everyone may share.'
So they came to the steep rock of lofty Cronus' son,*
and there he gave him a double treasure of prophecy:
first, to hear the voice that could not lie;*
and later, after the coming of bold Heracles,
a revered shoot from the stock of the Alcidae,*
and his institution of a festival, thronged by men,
for his father—the great foundation of the games—
he told him to set up an oracle at the very top of Zeus' altar.*   70
From that time the Iamid clan has been renowned in Hellas.
Prosperity has followed them; they honour noble deeds
and walk on a road where all can see them.
Their every action bears witness to this,
while the carping of other, rancorous men hangs over those
on whom, as they lead the race in the final lap of twelve,
revered Grace has shed a brilliant beauty.

If, Hagesias, your maternal ancestors,
living beneath the mountain of Cyllene,*
did in truth piously offer abundant prayers and sacrifices
to Hermes, herald of the gods, whose charge it is
to watch over the games and the contests' outcome,
and who holds Arcadia in honour, land of brave men;   80
then, son of Sostratus, it is he who with his deep-thundering
   father
has brought about your good fortune.

On my tongue I feel a sharp whetstone:
willingly, I am drawn on by lovely breaths of song.
My mother's mother was Stymphalian Metope,*
fair as a flower, who bore Thebe, driver of horses,
from whose enchanting spring I shall drink
while I weave an intricate song for spear-warriors.

Now, Aeneas,* exhort your companions
first to proclaim Hera Parthenia,*
and then to see if my truthful words
can deflect that ancient jibe, 'Boeotian pig';*   90
for you are an upright envoy,
a message-stick of the fair-haired Muses,*
a sweet mixing-bowl of loud-echoing songs.
Tell them to remember Syracuse and Ortygia,*
where Hieron rules with untainted sceptre and straight
     counsels,
honouring crimson-footed Demeter
and keeping the festival of her daughter* of the white horses,
and the feast of mighty Zeus on Aetna.*
Hieron is known to sweet-voiced lyres and songs;
may passing time not shatter his prosperity,
but may he with gracious affection welcome Hagesias' revel
as it returns, home from home, leaving Stymphalus' walls,
mother-city of Arcadia rich in flocks.   100

On a stormy night it is wise to drop two anchors from
     a swift ship.
May some friendly god grant a glorious destiny to both.
Lord, master of the sea,* husband of Amphitrite of the
     gold spindle,
grant them a straight passage, free from trouble,
and swell to fruition the pleasing flower of my songs.

OLYMPIAN 7

For Diagoras of Rhodes, winner in the boxing

As when a man takes a cup in his wealthy hand,
foaming inside with the dew of the vine,
and offers it to his young son-in-law—
a cup which is the golden crown of his possessions—
and toasts his exchange of homes, from one to another,
both to mark the feast and to honour his new kin,
and thus makes him envied in his friends' eyes
because of his marriage, a well-matched meeting of minds;
so in sending to prizewinners in the games a stream of nectar,
gift of the Muses and sweet fruit of my mind,
I propitiate them,* victors at Olympia and Delphi.   10

Happy is the man embraced by good report.
The charm of poetry, often set to the sound of the
      sweet-toned lyre
and the many-voiced pipe, gives vigour to life,
and looks kindly now on one and now on another.

And so to the accompaniment of both these instruments
I have come ashore with Diagoras, singing of Rhodes,*
      his island home,
child of Aphrodite and bride of Helios,
to praise this giant of a man, a straight fighter,
who has won a crown for boxing by Alpheus' river and
      at Castalia,*
and also to celebrate his father Damagetus, friend of justice.
Their home is an island of three cities,* close to a cape
      of broad Asia,
set among Argive spear-fighters.

My hope is to make known a true account, starting from
      Tlapolemus,   20
of their shared origin with the powerful race of Heracles.
On Tlapolemus' side they claim descent from Zeus,*
and on their mother's from Amyntor, father of Astydameia.

Over men's minds hang countless errors:
it is impossible to discover what best can happen to man,
both now and at the end. To illustrate:
Tlapolemus, this land's founder, once at Tiryns   30
struck Alcmene's* bastard brother Licymnius with a staff of
    hard olive
as he left Midea's* chamber, and killed him in a fit of anger.
Even a wise man can be led astray by derangement of the mind.
So Tlapolemus went to consult the god,
and the golden-haired one spoke from his fragrant shrine,
telling him to sail from Lerna's* shore straight to an island
    pasture,*
where once the great king of the gods
had sent down a shower of golden snow on to a city,
when by Hephaestus' art and a stroke of his bronze-forged axe
Athene sprang from the top of her father's head, yelling her
    monstrous war-cry,
and Heaven shuddered at her, and mother Earth.

Then it was that Hyperion's son, who brings light to mortals,
instructed his dear sons to be sure to fulfil a future
    obligation: 40
to be the first to erect a prominent altar to the goddess Athene,
to institute a sacrifice and so to warm the heart
of the virgin spear-thunderer and of her father.

Reverence, child of forethought, shoots excellence and joy
    into men's hearts;
but for all that an unexpected cloud of forgetfulness comes
    over them
and drags their minds away from the straight path of action.
And so it was they went up, but did not take with them the
    seeds of bright flame,
but established on the acropolis a sacred grove with fireless
    offerings.
Zeus called up a tawny-coloured cloud and rained abundant
    gold on them,   50
and the grey-eyed goddess* herself gave them every kind
    of craft,
so that they surpassed all mortals in the ingenuity of their hands.

In their streets stood statues like living and moving beings,
and their fame spread far abroad; for in an expert craftsman
skill flourishes when it is without artifice.

Ancient tales of men relate that when Zeus and the
   immortal gods
were giving out portions of the earth,
Rhodes had not yet appeared in the open sea
but lay hidden in its salty depths.
In his absence no one had allotted the sun-god Helios a share,
and so they left him, a revered god, without a portion
   of land.   60
He complained of this to Zeus, who set about recasting
   the lots,
but Helios stopped him; he saw, he said,
a land rising from the depths of the grey sea,
a land fruitful for men, and bountiful to their flocks.
At once Helios ordered Lachesis* of the golden headband
to raise her hands and to observe the gods' great oath,
and to undertake with Cronus' son that where the land
   had risen
to the bright upper air it should for all time be his prize and
   possession.
And so it fell out: the chief words of his speech were fulfilled,
and an island sprang up from the watery sea,
and Helios, father of the sun's piercing rays,
lord of fire-breathing horses, now holds it as his own.   70

Later he coupled with the nymph Rhodos and had by her
   seven sons,
who inherited from him the wisest minds among men of
   former times.
One sired Camirus, and Ialysus his first-born, and Lindus;
these shared out their ancestral land in three ways,
and each held his apportioned city apart, which now bear
   their names.

Here was established for Tlapolemus, lord of the men
   of Tiryns,
sweet requital for his miserable ill-fortune, as if he were a god:*

a procession, reeking with the smoke of sacrificed beasts,   80
and games* where men are judged for prizes.
In these Diagoras* has twice been crowned with garlands,
and has won four times at the famous Isthmus,
time after time at Nemea, and in rocky Athens.
The bronze* at Argos came to know him well,
as did the prizes in Arcadia and at Thebes,
and Boeotia's seasonal games, and Pellene,
as did Aegina, where he won six times;
and Megara, with its stone record of victory, tells the
    same story.

Father Zeus, lord of Atabyrion's* mountain ridges,
I pray you honour the custom of the Olympic victor's hymn,
and the man whose fists have won him success.
Grant him popular respect among his townsmen and with
    strangers,   90
for he walks on a straight road which abhors arrogant pride,
and has learnt well the lesson which his upright mind,
inherited from noble ancestors, has laid down for him.
Do not obscure the lineage which he shares with Callianax.*
Truly, when the Eratidae celebrate the city too holds festival.
But in one short span of time winds quickly shift direction,
veering back and forth.

OLYMPIAN 8

For Alcimedon of Aegina, winner in the boys' wrestling

Mother of gold-crowned games, Olympia, queen of truth,
where men who are seers interpret burnt offerings*
and test the mind of Zeus of the flashing thunderbolt,
to see if he has any word for men who struggle in their hearts
to win the rewards of excellence, and respite from their labours;
for men's prayers are fulfilled in accordance with their piety.
O wooded grove of Pisa beside the Alpheus,
I pray you welcome this victory revel, garlanded with crowns;   10
great for ever will be the glory of the man who is honoured
    by your prize.
Good fortune comes to men in different ways,
and many are the paths to god-aided success.

Timosthenes, destiny has allotted your clan to Zeus as its
    protector,*
who has brought you fame at Nemea, and has made your
    brother Alcimedon
an Olympic victor beside the hill of Cronus.
Handsome to look upon, his deeds matched his beauty;*
by his victory in the wrestling match   20
he proclaimed Aegina of the long oars as his fatherland,
where Themis* the Saviour, throned beside Zeus, Protector
    of Strangers,
is especially honoured among men.
When much hangs in the balance and it inclines this way
    and that,
a man may wrestle hard to make a straight, apt judgement;
but some ordinance of the immortals has established this
    sea-bound land
as a divine pillar of strength for strangers from every region.
May future time never grow weary of this work.

It is a land held in trust for the Dorian people,   30
from the time of Aeacus, who was summoned by Leto's son*
and by wide-ruling Poseidon to help them build Troy's walls

as they prepared to crown it with defences;
for it was fated that at war's onset Troy would in city-sacking
    battles
breathe forth gusts of angry smoke.
When the city was nearly built, three grey serpents tried
    to leap onto the wall;
two fell back in terror and died there and then,
but one leapt over with a triumphant cry.   40
Apollo pondered this adverse omen, and at once spoke:
'Hero Aeacus, Pergamus* will fall at the point where your
    hands have worked;
this is what the vision sent by the loud-thundering son
   of Cronus means to me.
Your descendants will have a hand in this:
it will begin in the first and fourth generations.'*
So the god spoke clearly, and in haste drove his team off
    towards the Xanthus,*
to the Amazons with their fine horses, and to the Ister.
But Poseidon the trident-wielder* urged his swift chariot
towards the sea-lapped Isthmus, returning Aeacus home
    behind his golden mares,   50
while he himself went on to visit the mountain ridge of
    Corinth, famous for its festivals.

Nothing will ever please all men equally.
If my song has raced on to tell of Melesias'* fame, trainer of
    beardless boys,
let not envy hurl a jagged stone at me;
I shall also speak of a like success won at Nemea,
and another there among men in the pancration.
In truth, teaching comes more easily to the man who
    already knows,
and not to be prepared beforehand is stupidity,   60
for the minds of the unpractised are insubstantial things.
But that man beyond all others can tell of his own successes,
and the best way to advance the man
who desires to win longed-for glory from the holy games.
And so now Alcimedon has brought him the honour of
    his thirtieth victory.

With good fortune from the gods, and because he did not
  fail his manhood,
he has shifted from himself onto the limbs of four boys
the bitterest of returns,* the jeering tongues, and the skulking
  journey home.
He has breathed into his father's father the strength to wrestle
  with old age.   70
Truly, the man who knows success forgets Hades.

But I must rouse my memory, and tell of the supreme
  achievement of hands
which brought victory to the Blepsiad clan,* the sixth crown
  to adorn them,
given at the games where men win garlands;
even the dead have a share in duly enacted rites,
and the dust does not hide from them their kinsmen's
  prized success.   80
Hearing from Hermes' daughter, the goddess of good news,
Iphion will tell his uncle Callimachus* of the glittering
  distinction
Zeus has granted their family at Olympia.
May Zeus be glad to heap glory upon glory for them,
and shield them from painful disease.
I pray he will not allot them a doubtful share of good
  things,
but will grant them a trouble-free life,
and cause them and their city to grow to greatness.

OLYMPIAN 9

For Epharmostus of Opus, winner in the wrestling

Archilochus' song,* the loud high triple hymn of victory,
    chanted at Olympia,
was good enough to conduct Epharmostus past
    Cronus' hill,*
when he revelled in triumph with his close companions.
But scatter* now from the Muses' far-shooting bow
a shower of arrows towards Zeus of the crimson lightning
and towards the holy hill of Elis,
which once the Lydian hero Pelops won as Hippodameia's
    splendid dowry.*   10
Shoot too a sweet feathered shaft towards Pytho.*
Your words will not fall to the ground when you make the
    lyre vibrate
in honour of the wrestling skill of a man from famous Opus,
as you praise the city and her son. For fate has allotted Opus
    to Themis
and to her renowned daughter Eunomia,* preserver of cities,
and it thrives on the strength of its people's deeds
by your waters, Castalia,* and by the streams of Alpheus.
And so the finest of crowns won in that place
glorify the Locrians' mother-city, famed for its beautiful
    trees.   20

As for me, when I shed lustre on that dear city with my
    blazing songs,
faster than a thoroughbred horse or a winged ship
I shall spread this news far and wide,
if only by some fortune-driven skill I can cultivate
choice flowers in the garden of the Graces;*
it is they who allot pleasures, but only by divine agency
do men become noble and wise.

How else could Heracles* have shaken his club against
    Poseidon's trident   30
when the god stood before Pylos and pressed him hard?

Or when Phoebus with his silver bow fought him and pressed
  him equally hard?
Nor did Hades hold back from brandishing his staff at him,
the staff with which he escorts the mortal bodies of the dead
to his hollow streets below.

But, my mouth, fling this story from me,
for to speak ill of the gods is a depraved art,
and loud untimely boasting sounds in harmony with
  madness.
Do not babble of such things;
keep war and fighting completely separate from the
  immortal gods.   40
Rather lend your tongue to Protogeneia's city,*
where by a decree of Zeus of the flashing thunderbolt
Pyrrha and Deucalion came down from Parnassus and built
  their first home,
and without intercourse created a single race from stones,
and therefore they are called a people.*
Awake for them a clear-sounding path of poetry.
Praise wine that is old, but for songs pick flowers that
  are new.

Now, men say that once a mass of water deluged the dark earth,   50
but by Zeus' artifice a backwash suddenly drained the
  flood away;
and from these people first came your bronze-shielded forebears,
sons of the daughters of Iapetus'* race and of Cronus'
  powerful sons,
kings for ever in their own land—until the lord of Olympus
carried off Opus' daughter from the land of the Epeians,*
and coupled with her in a secret place in Maenalus'* dales.
Later he gave her to Locrus, so that time should not ruin him
by awarding him a childless fate.   60
Locrus' wife was carrying a mighty seed in her,
and the hero's heart was gladdened to see his counterfeit son;
he gave him the name of his mother's father,*
and he grew to be a man beyond telling in beauty and
  great deeds,*
and Locrus gave him his city and people to rule over.

To him came strangers from Argos, from Thebes, from
    Arcadia and from Pisa;
but above all these settlers he honoured Menoetius, son of
    Actor and Aegina,   70
he whose son* went with Atreus' sons to the plain of
    Teuthras,*
and alone stood firm beside Achilles when Telephus routed
    the strong Danaans
and stormed their sea-going ships; and so discerning men
    saw and understood
Patroclus' forceful spirit. From that time Thetis' son*
advised him never to take his stand in the murderous battle
far away from his own man-slaying spear.

May I find the appropriate words to set out in the
    Muses' chariot,   80
and may resolution and abundant power accompany me.
Impelled by his success and by the ties of guest-friendship,
I came to honour Lampromachus'* Isthmian crown,
when on the same day both men* were victorious.
Later, there were two more joyful occasions for him
at the gates of Corinth,* and others for Epharmostus in the
    valley of Nemea.
At Argos he won glory among men, and at Athens as a boy;
and what a contest he endured at Marathon,
where, deprived of the chance to challenge beardless boys,
he competed with older men for silver cups!   90
Without falling himself he threw men by nimble shifting feints,
and left through the ring of spectators to noisy shouts,
young and handsome and the winner of handsome victories.
And again, he won admiration among the people of Parrhasia
at the festival for Lycaean Zeus,* and also at Pellana*
where he won a warm antidote to cold winds.
Iolaus'* tomb and coastal Eleusis are true witnesses of his
    glorious deeds.

Natural talents are the best in every way.   100
Many have taken lessons in prowess,
trying their utmost to achieve distinction;
but without a god's help every achievement

is best passed over in silence.
Some roads reach further than others,
and no single regime will develop us all.
All skills lie on a steep path; but when you give him this prize
raise a loud and confident shout that this man was with
    divine help   110
born with quick hands and agile legs, and with courage
    in his eyes.
At your feast, Ajax son of Ileus,* he has set on your altar
    a victor's crown.

For Hagesidamus of Western Locri, winner in the boys' boxing

Read me the name of the Olympic victor, Archestratus' son,
where it is written in my mind,
for I owe him a sweet song and have forgotten it.
Come, Muse, and you too, Truth, daughter of Zeus,*
and with an amending hand keep me from the charge of
breaking my word and wronging a friend.
For the future has caught up with me from afar,
and shamed me for my deep indebtedness.
But payment with interest can free me from the sharpness of
    that reproach;
as a rolling wave washes a tumbling pebble down the beach,   10
so I shall fulfil our contract and win a favour between friends.

Strict integrity rules the city of the Western Locrians,
and they pay heed to Calliope* and brazen Ares.
Even all-powerful Heracles was beaten back in battle with
    Cycnus.*
So now let Hagesidamus, boxing victor at the Olympic games,
give thanks to Ilas,* as Patroclus did to Achilles.*
If a man is born for success, another may with a god's help   20
sharpen his edge and drive him towards prodigious feats of
    glory;
and without exertion few have won joy,
which is a radiance in men's lives beyond all deeds.

The ordinances of Zeus have roused me
to sing of that special competition with its six altars*
which Heracles once established beside the ancient tomb of
    Pelops.
He had killed Cteatus, Poseidon's handsome son, and
    Eurytus* too,
to compel payment from Augeas for the menial service he
    did him—
willingly done, though Augeas was reluctant to pay him.
In a copse below Cleonae he lay in wait for them,   30

and on the road he slew these haughty Moliones,
because before this they had crushed his Tirynthian army
while it lay encamped in the dales of Elis.
And indeed soon afterwards the Epeian king, betrayer of
    guests,
saw his rich homeland subside under pitiless fire and blows
    of iron
into a deep trough of calamity.
Conflict with those who are stronger cannot be avoided.   40
So Augeas too at the end through his folly fell into captivity
and could not escape a sheer descent into death.

Then Zeus' mighty son gathered his whole army and all
    its plunder at Pisa,
and there measured out a sacred enclosure in honour of
    his great father.
He fenced the Altis* round and marked it off in an
    open space,
designated the plain around as a resting place for meals,
and honoured the Alpheus along with the twelve chief gods.
He gave the hill of Cronus its name; for before that time,   50
when Oenomaus was king, it had had no name,
but was covered deep in snow.
At this first-born ceremony the Fates too stood close by,
as did Time,* the only arbiter of absolute truth.
Time as it travels onward has clearly revealed
how Heracles divided up the spoils of war
and made an offering of the choicest portion,
and how he then founded the four-year festival
with the first Olympiad and its victorious triumphs.

Who then won the first fresh crown with hands, feet
    or chariot,   60
planting glory in the games in his thoughts and winning it
    by his deeds?
Licymnius' son Oeonus ran best in the straight stretch of the
    stadion race,
he who had come from Midea, at the head of his army.
In the wrestling, Echemus brought glory to Tegea.
Doryclus, whose city was Tiryns, won the boxing prize,

and in the four-horsed chariot race Samus of Mantinea.*   70
Halirothius' son Phrastor hit the mark with his javelin,
while Niceus whirled the stone in his hand and threw it
    beyond all others;
a great shout burst forth from the crowd,
and the lovely light of the moon's fair face made the
    evening bright.
The whole precinct rang with hymns of praise, sung at the
    joyful feast.

So, following this ancient example, we shall in turn sing a song
that takes its name from proud victory, extolling
the thunder and fiery bolt of Zeus, the noise-awakener,   80
the blazing lightning that accompanies every triumph.
Seductive melodies will respond to the pipe's reed,
songs which have at last come to light by famous Dirce.*

But just as the heart of a man, now far from youth,
is warmed with love for the longed-for son his wife has
    borne him—
for when wealth passes into the charge of a stranger,
a man from abroad, it torments a dying man—   90
so, Hagesidamus, a man who has done noble deeds
and reached the house of Hades without a song to praise him
has wasted his breath and won but little pleasure from his toil.
But on you the sweet-toned lyre and tuneful pipe are
    shedding fame,
and the Pierian daughters of Zeus* spread your glory far afield.

And I have eagerly added my support to the famous people
    of Locri,
showering their city of fine men with honey.
I have sung the praises of Archestratus' handsome son,
    whom I saw   100
victorious by the strength of his hands on that day near
    Olympia's altar;
beautiful to look upon, and endued with that youthfulness
    which once,
through the help of the Cyprus-born goddess,
saved Ganymede* from pitiless death.

OLYMPIAN 11

For Hagesidamus of Western Locri, winner in the boys' boxing

There is a time when men's greatest need is for winds,
and another for the waters of heaven, rainy children of
   the clouds.
But if a man wins success by his own efforts,
then honey-sweet songs are a prelude to later words of praise,
and a sure pledge of great achievements to come.
For Olympic victors, such praise is stored up beyond the reach
   of envy.
My tongue wishes to shepherd this praise;
but it is only through a god's agency
that a man's poetic skill grows to fruition.   10

Hagesidamus, son of Archestratus,
you should know that to extol your boxing victory
I shall add a sweet-voiced adornment to your crown of
   golden olive,
and thus honour the people of Western Locri.
Muses, join in their triumphal revels;
I promise it will be no inhospitable folk,
nor people unacquainted with beauty that you will meet,
but men highly skilled in poetry, and fine spearmen too.
Truly, neither the ruddy fox nor the loud-roaring lion
can change its inborn nature.   20

OLYMPIAN 12

For Ergoteles of Himera, winner in the long-distance race

Saviour Fortune, daughter of Zeus the Deliverer,* I pray to you:
watch over Himera and keep its strength secure.
For it is you who guide swift ships on the open sea,
and on land order tumultuous battles and counsel-giving
    assemblies.
But men's hopes are tossed up and down
as they voyage through waves of empty lies.
No man on earth has yet found out from the gods
a sure token of things to come;
man's perception is blinded as to the future.
Many things fall out for men in ways they do not expect: 10
sometimes their hoped-for pleasure is thwarted,
sometimes, when they have encountered storms of pain,
their grief changes in a moment to profound joy.

Son of Philanor, the glory that your swift feet have brought you
would have shed its leaves ingloriously,*
like a cock that fights only in its native yard,
had not factional strife robbed you of Cnossus, your homeland.
But, Ergoteles, now you have been crowned at Olympia,
once too at the Isthmus and twice at Pytho,
you bring fame* to the Nymphs' warm springs
and live in a land that is now your own.

OLYMPIAN 13

*For Xenophon of Corinth, winner of the short sprint race
and the pentathlon*

Praising the house that is three times victor at Olympia,
one kindly to its townsmen and hospitable to strangers,
will lead me to learn of prosperous Corinth,
gateway to Poseidon's isthmus,* city of brilliant young men.
There live Good Order and her sister Justice, a secure
    foundation for cities,
and Peace, nurtured with them, dispenser of wealth for men:
golden daughters of Themis* of good counsel,
eager to protect the city from Insolence, loose-mouthed
    mother of Excess.*   10
I have good things to tell,
and an honest confidence impels my tongue to speak:
inborn character cannot be concealed.

To you, sons of Aletes,* the many-flowered Seasons* have
    often granted victory's glory,
when, at the peak of your achievements, you triumphed
    at the sacred games;
often they have put ancient expertise into your men's hearts.
Everything looks back to its inventor:
from where did the delights of Dionysus come, and the
    dithyramb* that wins the ox prize?
Who added the guiding bit to the harness of horses?   20
Who set the twin kings of birds* on the temples of the gods?
Among this people the sweet-voiced Muse thrives,
and Ares in its young men's death-dealing spears.

Father Zeus on high, wide-ruling lord of Olympia,
do not for ever look with jealousy on my words,
but shield this people from harm
and give a fair wind to Xenophon's heaven-sent fortune.
Welcome this ritual celebration, honouring the crowns he
    brings from Pisa's plain,
victor in both the pentathlon and the stadion-race;   30

he has accomplished what no mortal man has reached before.
When he appeared at the Isthmian games two wreaths of
  wild celery
crowned his head, nor will Nemea tell a different story.
The brilliance of his father Thessalus' racing feet
is recorded by the waters of Alpheus,
and at Delphi he won fame in the double and single
  stadion-race in one day.
In the same month at rocky Athens one swift-footed day
crowned his head with prizes for three splendid victories,
and seven times was he honoured at the Hellotian* games.   40
As for Poseidon's festival* between the seas, it would need
  longer songs
to do justice to his father Ptoeodorus,* and to Terpsias
  and Eritimus.
Touching your family's victories at Delphi, or in the
  lion's haunts,*
I must contend with many who tell of the great number
  of their successes;
how indeed could I accurately number pebbles on the seashore?

Each thing is attended by due measure, and to understand this
  brings the greatest profit.
I am a private passenger on a public voyage,   50
and when I speak of the talents of their forefathers and their
  heroic deeds in war
I shall give no false account of the people of Corinth:
such as Sisyphus,* subtle and inventive as a god,
or Medea,* saviour of the ship Argo and its crew,
putting her own marriage before her father's wishes.

Again, in time past before the walls of Dardanian Troy
they showed by their courage they could decide the
  battles' issue,
one way or the other: some trying with Atreus' dear sons*
to win back Helen, others striving in every way to stop them;
for the Danaans trembled at the coming from Lycia
  of Glaucus,*   60
who claimed among them that his ancestor had ruled
  in Peirene's* city,

where there was a palace and a rich estate that were his.
He it was who, in his desire to harness Pegasus, the snaky
　　Gorgon's son,
suffered much near the spring—at least until the maiden
　　goddess Pallas
brought to him a bit with its golden headstall,
and his dream at once turned to waking vision.* She said:
'Are you asleep, prince of Aeolus' race? Come, take this
　　charmer of horses,*
sacrifice a white bull to your father the horse-tamer*
　　and show it to him.'
So it seemed to him that the maiden of the dark aegis had
　　spoken to him as he slept.　　　　　　　　　　　　　　　70
He sprang to his feet and seized the marvellous bit that
　　lay beside him,
and joyfully sought out the seer of the place, Coeranus' son,*
and explained all that had happened in the dream:
how he had slept all night on the goddess's altar as she had
　　instructed,
and how the daughter of Zeus the thunderbolt-hurler
had herself given him the spirit-taming gold.*
The seer told him to obey the dream as fast as he could:
he should sacrifice a strong-footed beast to the wide-ruling
　　Earth-holder　　　　　　　　　　　　　　　　　　　　80
and then at once set up an altar to Athene, goddess of horses.
Even things beyond oath and hope are easily fulfilled by the
　　gods' power.
And so mighty Bellerophon reached out
and put the soothing charm about the winged horse's muzzle,
　　and subdued it.
Quickly he mounted, and armed in bronze began to wave
　　his weapon in sport.
Later, with his horse's help, he swooped down
from the chill gulfs of the empty upper air
and laid low the army of the Amazons, female archers,
and the fire-breathing Chimaera, and the Solymi.*　　　　90
About his fate* I shall keep silent;
but his horse is still lodged in Zeus' ancient stables on
　　Olympus.

But as I whirl my many javelins on their straight course
I must not hurl weapons from my hand so as to miss the mark,
for I have come as a willing ally of the Muses on their
   shining thrones,
and to help the clan of Oligaethidae.
As for their victories at the Isthmus and Nemea,
a short word from me will make the sum total plain;
and as a true sworn witness, the excellent herald's
   sweet-voiced cry,   100
uttered sixty times at both games, will add its confirmation.
Their victories at Olympia have, it seems, already been told,
and as for those in the future, I shall praise them when
   they come.
I have my hopes for now, though the outcome lies with
   the god.
If, with divine help, their clan continues to prosper,
we can leave it to Zeus and Enyalius* to bring about success.
Their victories under the brow of Parnassus were six,
and there were the same number at Argos and at Thebes.
Touching those in Arcadia's valleys, the regal altar of the
   Lycaean* will bear witness,
as too will Pellana and Sicyon and Megara,
and the well-fenced precinct of the Aeacids,* Eleusis and
   gleaming Marathon,   110
Euboea, and the fine rich cities under high-ridged Aetna.

If you search through all Hellas you will find more victories
   than the eye can see.
Come, swim out* with nimble feet. Zeus the Accomplisher,
grant them modesty and the sweet pleasures of good fortune.

OLYMPIAN 14

For Asopichus of Orchomenus, winner of the short sprint race

O Graces, possessing the waters of Cephisus* as your own,
you who live in a land of fine horses, queens of gleaming
    Orchomenus,
celebrated in song, guardians of the ancient race of Minyans;*
hear me when I pray to you.
Through you all pleasures come to men,
whether a man is a skilled poet, or handsome, or famous.
Without the stately Graces not even the gods can order
    dances or feasts;
they are the stewards of all things in heaven,   10
and have set their thrones next to Pythian Apollo, lord
    of the golden bow,
and they hold in reverence the everlasting dignity of their
    Olympian father.
Lady Radiance, and you, Good Cheer, lover of song,
children of the mightiest of the gods, hear me now;
and you, Festivity, who delight in song,
as you watch this revelling procession, stepping lightly at
    his good fortune,
for I have come singing of Asopichus,
composing in my accustomed way in the Lydian mode,*
because with your aid the city of the Minyans has triumphed
    at Olympia.
Go now, Echo, to the black-walled house of Persephone*   20
and take this glorious news to his father Cleodamus,
so that when you see him you may say of his son
that in Pisa's famous valley he has crowned his youthful head
with winged garlands from the games that bring renown.

PYTHIANS

PYTHIAN 1

For Hieron of Aetna, winner of the chariot race

Golden lyre, possession and colleague of Apollo and the
    violet-haired Muses;
to you the dancer's step listens as it begins the bright
    celebration,
and the singers obey your directions when with quivering
    strings
you strike up the preludes which lead to the dance.
You stifle even the warlike thunderbolt of ever-flowing fire;
and the eagle, king of birds, sleeps on the sceptre of Zeus,
folding his swift wings to his sides,
because you have poured a dark cloud over his bent head,
a sweet shutter for his eyelids;
in sleep he flexes his supple back, spellbound by your
    throbbing music.   10
And violent Ares lays aside his cruelly pointed spear
and warms his heart in sleep,
for your shafts charm even the hearts of gods,
through the skill of Leto's son* and the Muses with their
    deep-folded robes.

But creatures unloved by Zeus shudder when they hear the
    Pierians'* voice,
whether on earth or in the relentless sea;
and the one who lies in dreadful Tartarus, hundred-headed
    Typhos,*
enemy of the gods, nurtured once by the far-famed cave
    of Cilicia,
but now sea-fronting cliffs over Cumae press down on his
    shaggy breast,
and the pillar of snow-covered Aetna, rearing to heaven,
year-long nurse of freezing snow, pins him down.   20

From its depths spew sacred founts of fire that cannot be
    approached;
by day rivers pour forth lurid streaks of smoke,
and by night a crimson rolling flame sweeps down rocks,
which crash into the sea's broad expanse.
That monster spouts forth terrifying torrents of
    Hephaestus' fire—
a prodigious portent to behold, and a wonder for visitors
    to hear.
Such a thing is imprisoned between Aetna's dark-wooded
    peaks and its plain,
and the bed he lies on gouges and galls the whole length
    of his back.

Grant, O Zeus, grant that I may please you:
watcher over this mountain, forehead of a
    fertile land,
whose neighbour namesake city* was made glorious by its
    famous founder
when at Pytho's racecourse the herald proclaimed it,
telling of Hieron's splendid victory in the chariot race.

For men who sail in ships the first sign of favour as
    they embark
is the rising of a following wind, because then there is
    a fair chance
that they will enjoy a safe return too at the end of
    their voyage.
And this saying, on the back of such success, brings hope
that the city will be famed in future for crowns won
    with horses,
and renowned for its festivals of sweet music.
Phoebus,* lord of Lycia and ruler of Delos,
lover of Castalia's spring at Parnassus,
be willing to store my wish in your heart
and make this a land of brave men.

All mortal achievement stems from the gods' designs:
thus are born skilled poets and men of strong hands and great
    eloquence.

30

40

Eager to praise that famous man,* I hope I do not, as one
    might say,
throw the bronze-tipped javelin I spin with my hand outside
    the field of play,
but surpass my competitors by the length of my cast.
May his whole life continue to steer happiness and the gift
    of wealth
towards him, bringing him forgetfulness of past hardship.
Time will surely remind him of the battles*
where he stood his ground with unflinching spirit,
when with the gods' help he and his family won honour
such as no Hellene has ever reaped—a lordly crown of riches.   50

And now indeed he went to war like Philoctetes,
compelling even a proud man to fawn on him as a friend.
Men say that godlike heroes came to fetch him, Poeas' archer son,
from Lemnos, exhausted by his wound; and so
he sacked Priam's city and brought the Danaans' labours to
    an end.
He walked with a sick body, but this was how it was fated.
Just so may the god preserve Hieron in time to come,
giving him the opportunity to grasp what he desires.

And, Muse, let me persuade you to sing too in
    Deinomenes'* house
of the reward for the four-horsed chariot, for his father's
    victory is no alien joy.
Come, let us devise a welcome song for Aetna's king,   60
for whom Hieron founded that city with god-built freedom,
according to the ordinances of Hyllus' rule;*
for the descendants of Pamphylus, and indeed of Heracles' sons,
who live under the heights of Taygetus,
desire as Dorians always to keep to the statutes of Aegimius.
They came down from Pindus and occupied Amyclae
    in prosperity,
and were renowned neighbours to the Tyndarids of the
    white horses,
and the fame of their spears increased.
Zeus, Accomplisher, grant that such a destiny may always
    hold good

for Aetna's citizens and kings beside the waters of Amenas,*
a true record on the lips of men.
For if you help him, a ruler who advises his son well   70
may by honouring his people turn them towards
   harmonious peace.

I pray you, son of Cronus, grant that the war-cry
   of Phoenicians and Etruscans
may stay at home, now that they have seen their
   insolent violence
bring lamentation on their fleet for what it endured at Cumae,
crushed by the Syracusan commander, who hurled their
   finest men
from their swift ships into the sea, and rescued Greece
   from harsh slavery.
From Salamis I shall earn the Athenians' thanks as payment,
and in Sparta for my tale of the battles before Cithaeron,*
where the Medes who shoot with curved bows were overcome.
But by the well-watered bank of Himera
my reward shall be for the song I have made for
   Deinomenes' sons,
which they earned by their courage when their enemies
   were overthrown.   80

If you should speak in keeping with the occasion,*
plaiting the threads of many matters into a brief whole,
men will find less fault with you;
for wearisome excess blunts the edge of keen expectancy,
and in their secret hearts men are especially oppressed
when they hear praise of other citizens.
Nevertheless, since it is better to be envied than pitied,
do not deviate from your noble course.
Steer your people with the rudder of justice,
and forge your tongue on the anvil of truth.

You know that even a trivial word can carry great influence,
if it leaps like a spark from your mouth.
You hold great wealth in trust, and there are many men
to bear reliable witness to your acts, for good or ill.
Retain the full vigour of your spirits,

and if it pleases you to hear that men always speak well of you 90
do not grow weary of spending,
but like a steersman let your sail out to catch the wind.

My friend, do not be taken in by unworthy use of wealth,
for the award of posthumous fame is the only testimony
that storytellers and poets can give to the lives of the dead.
Croesus' generous virtues do not fade,
but he who burnt men in his brazen bull, Phalaris,*
is dogged by an evil report throughout the world,
and no lyres in men's halls welcome him to the soft embrace
    of boys' voices.
Success is the best prize, and the next best destiny is a good
    reputation;
but the man who lights on both and holds them fast wins
    the highest crown. 100

PYTHIAN 2

For Hieron of Syracuse, winner of the chariot race

Syracuse, great city, sanctuary of Ares* who lives in the thick
    of war,
divine nurse of horsemen who delight in iron,
I come to you from gleaming Thebes bringing this song
which tells of an earth-shaking four-horse team:
how Hieron, possessor of fine chariots, won the prize,
and with far-shining wreaths crowned Ortygia,* home of
    river-goddess Artemis;*
not without her aid did he tame with gentle hands
those colts with their richly worked reins.
For it is the maiden goddess, delighting in the bow,
who with Hermes, god of the games, fits the bright harness
    with both hands,   10
when Hieron yokes his strong horses to the polished car
and to the chariot that governs the bit,
calling on the wide-ruling god, the trident-holder.*

As tribute to their success men pay kings sweet-sounding
    songs.
Often the men of Cyprus sing of Cinyras,*
whom golden-haired Apollo gladly befriended,
and who was Aphrodite's favourite priest;
for reciprocal favour is paid in return for deeds of friendship.
And you, son of Deinomenes, are extolled in front of her house
by a maiden of Western Locri,* because after desperate
    struggles of war
she now, because of your power, gazes out with confidence.   20

Ixion,* they say, whirling wildly on his wheel by the gods' decree,
speaks these words to mortals:
Repay your benefactor, always meeting him with gentle acts
    of recompense.
He learnt this lesson in unambiguous terms,
for though he had won an agreeable life with the friendly
    children of Cronus

he did not enjoy his happiness for long,
since in his crazy heart he conceived a passion for Hera,
whose duty it was to bring pleasure to the bed of Zeus.
Insolence drove him into presumptuous folly,
and he quickly suffered his deserts, earning exquisite
   torment for himself.   30
Two crimes brought punishment on this hero:
he was the first to pollute mortals with the taint of kindred
   bloodshed—
not without cunning—and once in the recesses of her great
   bedchamber
he made an attempt to rape the wife of Zeus.
One must always gauge everything by one's own station.
Illicit sexual passions hurl men into utter ruin,
and they also proved his undoing,
for—ignorant man—he pursued a lovely deception
   and coupled with a cloud,
which mimicked the shape of heaven's supreme goddess,
   the daughter of Cronus.
Zeus' ingenuity contrived this as a trap for him—a beautiful
   misfortune.   40

And so he earned his own ruin, bound to the four-spoked wheel.
Caught in inescapable bonds, he was given a message that
   touches us all.
That singular mother bore him a singular monstrous son
without the Graces' favour, one not honoured among men or
   in the gods' society.
She raised it and called it Centaurus,* and it mated with
   mares of Magnesia*
in the foothills of Pelion, from which sprang a remarkable brood,
resembling both its parents: the mother's parts below, and the
   father's above.

A god accomplishes his every plan as he intends—
a god, who can outstrip even the winged eagle
and overtake the dolphin of the sea,   50
who forces many a haughty mortal to yield while giving others
   eternal glory.
I must avoid the violent bite of slander;

in times long gone I have seen the censorious Archilochus*
    often suffering
because he fattened himself on harsh words of hatred.

Wealth allied to good fortune is the best destiny poetic wisdom
    can give.
You clearly possess this, and can display it with a liberal spirit,
ruler and master of many well-fortified streets and of
    a numerous people.
If anyone today says that another man of former times
    in Greece   60
was superior to you in possessions and reputation,
he is empty-minded, and wrestles to no purpose.
To proclaim your prowess I shall board a flower-garlanded ship.
In terrible wars youth is supported by boldness,
and I say that there too you have acquired your boundless glory,
on campaigns with horsemen and with foot-soldiers.
Your counsels, mature in your later years,
allow me to praise you freely on every account.

Farewell; this song is sent to you over the grey sea like
    Phoenician merchandise.
As for the other, the song of Castor* sung to Aeolian strings,
look favourably upon it, the splendour of the seven-stringed
    lyre, as you meet it.   70

You have learnt what kind of a person you are: now become
    that man.
In the eyes of children, as we know, the ape is a handsome
    thing—always handsome;
but Rhadamanthys* prospers because fate has allotted him
the excellent fruit of a sound mind, and in his heart
he takes no pleasure in the kind of deceptions
that always keep mortals company, through whisperers'
    artfulness.
Spreaders of slander cause irresistible harm to both parties,
for their natures are exactly those of foxes.
But what real gain comes from this kind of trickery?
None, for while the rest of the fisherman's gear does its work
    in the sea's depths

I am like a cork bobbing unsubmerged on its salt surface.   80
A dishonest citizen cannot utter weighty words in good
    men's company,
but such a man will fawn on everyone, weaving his webs
    of delusion.
I wish no part in his audacity. Let me be a friend to my friend,
but my enemy—since I am his enemy—I shall hunt down
like a wolf, tracking him here and there on zigzag paths.

In every polity the straight-speaking man is best—whether
    under a tyranny
or when the violent mob or the wise watch over it.
One should not fight against the god,
who now raises a man up and then again gives great glory
    to others.
But not even this thought cheers the minds of the envious,   90
who stretch the measuring line too tight
and so inflict a painful wound in their own heart
before they can achieve what they have devised in their minds.
It is best to accept the yoke on one's neck and bear it lightly;
truly, kicking against the goad makes for a slippery path.
May it be my fate to enjoy the approval of good men, and
    to keep their company.

PYTHIAN 3

For Hieron of Syracuse

If it is right for my tongue to speak this communal prayer,
I would wish that the now dead Chiron,* son of Philyra
and wide-ruling scion of Cronus son of Uranus, were still alive,
and that he were still lord in Pelion's valleys,
a wild untamed creature but with a heart that loved men—
just as he was when long ago
he reared that gentle deviser of limb-healing relief from pain,
Asclepius, the hero who protects men against every kind
    of disease.

Before the time had come for her to give birth to him
with the help of Eleithyia, attendant of mothers,
the daughter of Phlegyas* the horseman was brought low
in her bedchamber by the golden arrows of Artemis,   10
and went down to Hades' house by Apollo's devising.
The anger of Zeus' children is no slight thing.
Yet she in her mind's folly had rebuffed him,
and had agreed without her father's knowledge to another
    marriage,
though she had already lain with Phoebus of the unshorn hair
and was carrying the pure seed of the god.
She would not wait for the wedding feast to come,
nor the sound of the many-voiced bridal hymn
which a girl's unwedded companions chant in affectionate
    evening songs;*
but she was infatuated with far-off things—   20
a craving which many others have suffered.

There is among mankind a very foolish breed, who disdain
    familiar things
and look with longing at what is out of reach,
seeking the impossible with hopes that will never be fulfilled.
Such was the strong delusion which seized the mind of Coronis,
she of the lovely robes. She lay in the bed of an Arcadian stranger,
but she did not escape the one who watched her,

for though he was then in sheep-receiving Pytho
Loxias* lord of his temple was aware of her,
trusting in his omniscient mind, his unerring companion;
he has no truck with lies, and no mortal or god
can outwit him either in words or in deeds.   30

And so now, when he realized her impious duplicity,
that she was bedded with the stranger Ischys son of Elatus,
he sent his sister, wild with resistless anger, to Lacereia
beside the steep shores of Boebias,* where the girl lived.
A contrary doom struck her down and hurled her into disaster,
and many of her neighbours suffered and died with her;
a fire that starts from one spark can destroy a great forest.

But when her relatives had laid the girl inside a wall of wood
and the ravening brightness of Hephaestus had enveloped her,
then Apollo spoke: 40
'I can no longer bear in my heart to destroy my own offspring
in a most pitiful death, together with his mother's hard suffering.'
So he spoke, and in one stride reached the pyre
and caught up the child from the corpse;
and the burning flames opened a way for him.
He took the child and gave him to the centaur of Magnesia
to teach him how to cure men of their painful infirmities.

And so if any came to him with chronic sores as constant
     companions,
or with limbs wounded by the grey bronze or a far-flung stone,
or whose body was wasted by summer fever or winter cold,   50
he relieved them of their several pains and so restored them
     to health.
Some he treated with emollient incantations, others with potions,
and for others he applied salves all over their bodies,
while others he set back on their feet by surgery.

But even skill can become the prisoner of gain.
Gold displayed in the hand was a princely inducement
for even him to recall from death a man already in its grip.
The son of Cronus tore the breath from both in a moment,
and with his hands' heave the blazing thunderbolt dealt
     them death.

Men should seek from the gods only what is consistent
   with mortal minds,
knowing what lies before our feet, and the nature of
   our destiny.   60
Do not, my soul,* long for an immortal life,
but make the most of what you can realistically achieve.

If sagacious Chiron were still living in his cave,
and my sweet songs could somehow thrust a charm into
   his heart,
then I would surely have persuaded him
to grant us a healer of feverish diseases for mortals,
one named as a son of Leto's child or of his father.*
And I would have come by ship, slicing through the Ionian sea,
to the spring of Arethusa* to see my guest-friend of Aetna,
who governs the Syracusans as king; one gentle to his
   fellow citizens,   70
open-handed to the good, and a remarkable father to strangers.
If I had landed there, bringing him a double favour—
golden health, and a triumphant revel, brilliance added to the
   crowns
from the Pythian games which Pherenicus once won
   at Cirrha—*
I say I would have come to him as a light that shines brighter
than any star in the heaven, when I had crossed the deep sea.

But I wish to pray to the Mother, the revered goddess,
to whom, with Pan,* girls often sing before my door at night.
If you, Hieron, can understand the true meaning of sayings,   80
you will have learnt this lesson from men of old:
that for every blessing the immortals hand men a double grief.*
Fools cannot wear this with dignity but good men can,
by turning the better side outward.

But as for you, a happy fate awaits you,
for surely if great destiny looks favourably on anyone
it is on a ruler who leads his people.
But a secure life did not stay with Peleus, Aeacus' son, nor with
   godlike Cadmus;*
yet men say they enjoyed the greatest happiness of any mortal,

for they even heard the gold-capped Muses singing on the
    mountain,
and at seven-gated Thebes; the one when he wedded
    Harmonia,   90
and the other glorious Thetis, daughter of straight-counselling
    Nereus.
Moreover the gods feasted with both,
and they saw the kingly sons of Cronus on their golden thrones,
and received from them wedding gifts.
By Zeus' favour they put their former hardships behind them,
and lifted up their hearts with confidence.
But things changed with time, and later the painful
    sharp sufferings
of his three daughters deprived the one of part of his happiness,
though Father Zeus did come to the desirable bed of
    white-armed Thyone.
And the other's son, the only child immortal Thetis bore to
    him in Phthia,   100
lost his life in war to an arrow, and roused a lament among
    the Danaans
when his corpse was consumed by fire.

If a man holds to the path of truth in his mind
he must be content with whatever the blessed gods send him.
Gusts of soaring winds blow now this way, now that;
lasting prosperity does not visit men for long,
even when it has attended them with all its weight.
I shall be small when times are small, and great when they
    are great.
Whatever fortune comes my way I shall respect it with my mind
and nurture it according to my powers.
If a god should hold out luxurious wealth to me   110
I hope I shall use it to acquire glory in time to come.
It is from sonorous verses such as skilful poets constructed
that we know of Nestor and Lycian Sarpedon,* the talk of men.
Glory-giving songs cause excellence to abide for ages,
but few men find them easy to acquire.

PYTHIAN 4

For Arcesilas of Cyrene, winner of the chariot race

Today, my Muse, you must stand at the side of a friend,
Arcesilas, king of Cyrene of the fine horses,
so that with him in his victory revel you may swell the winds
  of song
which are owed to Leto's children* and to Pytho—
where once the priestess who sits near Zeus' golden eagles*
  foretold,
in Apollo's presence, that Battus would settle in fruitful Libya;
that he should now leave the holy island
and found a city of fine chariots* on that land's white breast,
and so fulfil, in the seventeenth generation,
the words Medea's immortal mouth once breathed out
  on Thera,
mistress of Colchis and mettlesome daughter of Aeetes.   10

Thus she spoke to the spearman Jason's demigod crew:
'Listen to me, sons of high-spirited men and gods:
I tell you that one day from this sea-beaten island
the daughter of Epaphus* will plant a root
from which cities revered by men will spring,
near the foundations of Zeus Ammon.*
In place of short-finned dolphins their people will raise
  swift horses,
and instead of oars they will handle reins
and chariots with the speed of the storm.

'This sign will bring it to pass
that Thera will become the mother-city of great cities: 20
the symbol which Euphamus once received
when he leapt from his ship's prow at Lake Tritonis'* outflow,
and a god in the likeness of a man gave him a clod of earth
as a guest-present; and Father Zeus, son of Cronus,
crashed out a thunderclap in confirmation,
at the time when he found us hanging the bronze-fluked anchor,
swift Argo's bridle, against the ship.

Before this, we had dragged our sea-going craft on to the shore
in accordance with my designs, and for twelve days
had been carrying it from Ocean over desert tracts of land.
It was then that the god drew near to us, alone,
having assumed the glorious appearance of a man of esteem.
His first words were friendly, such as hospitable men use   30
when they invite newly arrived strangers to a feast.
But the excuse of our sweet return home prevented us
    from staying.

'He said he was Eurypylus, son of the immortal Holder
and Shaker of the Earth.* He knew we were anxious to leave,
but straight away caught up some earth in his right hand
and pressed it on Euphamus as a makeshift guest-present.
The hero did not resist him, but jumped down onto the shore,
grasped his hand firmly in his own, and accepted the
    god-sent clod.
I hear that one evening it was washed off the ship by a wave
and fell into the sea and took its course over the watery
    expanse.   40
Many times indeed I had urged the servants who lighten
    our labour
to keep it safe, but their minds were forgetful;
and so the undying seed of spacious Libya
has been washed up on this island* before its time.

'For if Euphamus, kingly son of Poseidon tamer of horses,
whom Europa, Tityus' daughter, once bore to him by
    Cephisus' banks,
had returned home to holy Taenarus* and thrown it down
near the earth's portal to Hades,
the blood in the fourth generation of his children
would have taken possession of that broad mainland
with the Danaans; for at that time they are to rise up
and leave great Lacedaemon, and the Argive gulf,
    and Mycenae.
But as it is, he will find in the beds of foreign women*   50
a chosen race, who honoured by the gods will come to
    this island
and will father a man to be lord of those dark-clouded plains.

In time to come he will make a journey to Pytho's temple,*
and Phoebus in his gold-rich palace will remind him
      through oracles
to transport cities in ships to the rich precinct of Cronus' son
      by the Nile.'

Such were the oracular utterances of Medea.
And the godlike heroes stood in motionless silence,
awestruck as they listened to her deep counsel.

It was you, blessed son of Polymnastus, whom the
      oracle celebrated
in this speech, through the unsolicited cry of the Delphic bee.*   60
Three times she greeted you, and revealed you as Cyrene's
      destined king,
when you had enquired of her what release there might be
from the gods for your stammering speech. And so it turned out,
later, as it were at the height of red-flowering spring,
the eighth generation of his line flourishes in Arcesilas.
Apollo and Pytho have granted him renown
among surrounding peoples for his chariot racing.
As for me, I shall offer him to the Muses,
and with him the ram's all-golden fleece,
for it was when the Minyans* set sail in search of it
that god-sent honours were planted for them.

What caused them to begin their voyage?   70
What prospect of danger bound them with strong nails
      of adamant?
There was an oracle that Pelias* would die at the hands
of the lordly Aeolids, or by their inescapable intrigues.
A prophecy came to him that froze his wily heart,
one delivered at the mother's central navel-stone,* thick
      with trees,
that he should take all possible precautions
against the man with one sandal,
when he should come, a stranger or a fellow citizen,
from his mountain home to the sunlit land of famous Iolcus.

And indeed in time he did come: a striking man, carrying
      twin spears.

He wore two kinds of clothing:
native Magnesian* garments covered his splendid limbs, 80
and a leopard skin shielded him against the chilling rain.
His bright long hair was not shorn and lost,
but streamed down the whole length of his back.
Swiftly he strode into the marketplace and stood among the
    thronging crowd,
putting his unflinching purpose to the test.
They did not recognize him; but as they stood stunned one
    of them said:
'This surely cannot be Apollo, nor Aphrodite's husband*
of the bronze chariot; and men say the sons of Iphimedeia
died in bright Naxos—Otus, and you, daring king Ephialtes.
And certainly Tityus* was hunted down by Artemis'
    swift arrow, 90
shot from her invincible quiver, so that men might desire
to reach only those pleasures* which are within their power.'

While they talked among themselves in this way,
Pelias arrived at headlong speed in his polished mule-drawn car.
The moment he caught sight of the conspicuous single sandal
on the man's right foot he was dumbfounded,
but concealed his fear in his heart and said:
'What land do you claim as your own, stranger?
And what earth-born woman dropped you out of her
    grey womb?
Tell me your ancestry, and do not pollute it with
    repellent lies.' 100

He answered him with confident and mild words:
'I declare that I shall exemplify the teachings of Chiron,*
for I come from the cave of Chariclo and Philyra,
where the centaur's holy daughters reared me.
Twenty years I spent there, with never an untoward deed
or word to them, and now I have come to my home
to repossess my father's ancient privilege:
the kingship held unlawfully, which long ago
Zeus gave to Aeolus, leader of his people, and to his sons;
since I hear that the lawless Pelias has yielded to unjust thoughts

and has violently stripped it from my parents, the rightful
   rulers.   110
They, as soon as ever I saw the light, fearing the brutal insolence
of an arrogant ruler, arranged a gloomy funeral in the palace
as if I had died, and amid the keening of women
secretly sent me away wrapped in red swaddling clothes,
making the night the confidant of my journey,
and gave me to Chiron the son of Cronus to be raised.
So now you know the bare facts of my story.
Good citizens, show me clearly the palace of my fathers,
lords of white horses; for as Aeson's son I am a native here,
and it is to no alien land that I have come.
The divine beast called me by the name of Jason.'

So he spoke, and went into his home, and his father's eyes
   knew him,   120
and tears gushed forth from behind his aged eyelids,
and he rejoiced in his heart seeing his incomparable son,
   most handsome of men.
At the news of his coming Aeson's two brothers appeared,
Pheres from the nearby spring of Hypereis, and Amythaon
   from Messene.
And quickly Admetus and Melampus* too arrived,
full of kindly feeling towards their cousin.
While they feasted Jason welcomed them with gracious words,
offering them due hospitality and prolonging the entertainment
in all kinds of ways for fully five nights and days,   130
plucking the holy flower of festive enjoyment.
But on the sixth day he set out in sober words the whole
   story from the start,
and shared it with his kinsmen, and they sided with him.
At once he rose with them from their couches;
going to the palace of Pelias they entered quickly and took
   their stand.
When he heard them, lovely-haired Tyro's son met them in person.
In a soft voice Jason poured gentle words over him,
and so laid the foundation of wise speech:

'Son of Poseidon of the Rock, men's minds are all too quick
to applaud dishonest gain above the right course of action,   140

even though they will come to a hard reckoning on the
    morning after.
Still, you and I must control our passions with the rule of law,
and so weave happiness for the future.
You know what I am going to say:
Cretheus and reckless Salmoneus* were born to one
    heifer mother,
and we are descended in the third generation from them,
and look upon the might of the sun.
The Fates stand apart from kinsmen if there is enmity
    between them,
causing them to conceal their respect for one another.
It is not right for the two of us to divide up the great
    possessions
of our ancestors by means of sharp bronze swords or spears.
I surrender to you the sheep-flocks, the herds of tawny cattle,
and all the land which you have stolen from my parents
and now control, fattening up your wealth.   150
It does not grieve me that all this immoderately feeds
    your house;
but as for the sceptre of sole authority,
and the throne where Cretheus' son Aeson formerly sat
and handed down straight judgements to his horseman people—
yield these up to me, without hurt to either,
lest some new trouble arise for us as a result.'

So he spoke, and Pelias answered softly: 'I shall do as you say.
But old age is now my life's portion and keeps me company,
while the flower of your youth now swells in bloom,
and you have the power to dispel the anger of powers below
    the earth;
Phrixus* commands us to bring his spirit home,   160
by going to the palace of Aeetes and fetching here
the thick-fleeced hide of the ram by whose help he was
    once saved
from the open sea and from his stepmother's godless weapons.
A strange dream came to me and told me this.
I went to consult the oracle at Castalia*
to see if some search should be undertaken,

and it urges me to prepare a seagoing expedition as soon as
   possible.
Agree to perform this undertaking,
and I swear I shall surrender to you both kingship and sole rule.
May Zeus our common ancestor be our witness, that this is a
   mighty oath.'

So they willingly made this agreement, and parted.
But Jason himself forthwith sent heralds everywhere   170
to announce that a naval expedition was planned.
Without delay there came three sons* of Zeus the son of Cronus,
tireless in battle, whose mothers were glancing-eyed Alcmene
   and Leda;
also two long-haired men,* sons of the Earthshaker,
from Pylos and Taenarus, conscious of their reputation
   for valour;
thus was Euphamus' noble fame secured, and yours, mighty
   Periclymenus.
And sent by Apollo there came the lyre-player and father
   of song,
greatly admired Orpheus. Hermes of the golden staff
sent his twin sons for this task which had no end,
Echion and Erytus, exulting loudly in their youth.
From their homes in the foothills of Pangaeon*   180
came two swift men, Zetes and Calais, for their father Boreas,
lord of the winds, quickly sent them with a willing and
   cheerful heart—
two men whose backs both bristled with purple wings.
Hera kindled in these gods' sons an irresistible sweet desire
   for the ship Argo,
so that none of them was left behind at his mother's side
to brood over a life without danger, but each discovered
   among his fellows
the finest physic for his excellence, even in the face of death.

When the flower of seafarers landed at Iolcus,
Jason congratulated and marshalled them,
and the seer Mopsus, divining from birds and from
   sacred lots,
sent them on board with a good grace.   190

When they had hung their anchors up on the prow,
their chief Jason lifted a golden bowl in his hands,
and standing on the stern called upon Zeus, father of Heaven's
    inhabitants,
whose spear is the lightning, and upon the swing of the waves
to speed their way, and upon the winds and nights and days
and paths of the open sea to show them favour,
and bring them the longed-for destiny of a return home.
From the clouds an auspicious clap of thunder crashed in answer,
and vivid flashes of lightning burst forth.
Trusting in these signs from the god, the heroes took fresh heart;
and, voicing their joyful hopes, the seer called them to fall
    to their oars.   200
Under their fast-moving hands the tireless rowing advanced.
Sped on by the south wind's breezes, they reached the mouth
    of the Inhospitable Sea;*
there they established a precinct sacred to Poseidon, god
    of the sea,
and there was nearby a herd of reddish Thracian cattle
and a newly built altar of stone with a flat top.
About to launch themselves into deep danger, they prayed
    to the lord of ships
to escape from the irresistible motion of the Clashing Rocks.*
There were two of these, and they were alive, and rolled along
more swiftly than columns of deep-bellowing winds;   210
but this expedition of demigods finally brought about
    their end.

Then they came to the Phasis,* and fought with all their
    strength
against the dark-faced Colchians before Aeetes himself.
And there it was that the Cyprus-born goddess, mistress of
    sharpest arrows,
first brought from Olympus to men the speckled wryneck, the
    bird of frenzy,
and bound it helplessly to a four-spoked wheel.
She fully instructed Aeson's son in the skill of prayers and spells,
so that he might wrench Medea away from respect for
    her parents,

and so that desire for Hellas might with Persuasion's whip
unsettle her, whose heart was already aflame.
Quickly she showed him how to perform the tasks her father
     would set.   220
Mixing drugs with oil she concocted antidotes to agonizing pain
and gave them to him to smear on himself;
and they vowed they would be joined to each other in the
     sweet union of marriage.

But when Aeetes had set before all a plough of adamant,
and oxen which breathed flames of burning fire from their
     tawny jaws
and which tore up the ground with the pawing of their
     bronze hoofs,
he controlled them and forced them single-handed under
     the yoke-strap.
The furrows stretched in straight lines as he drove them on,
splitting the back of the clodded earth six feet deep.
Then he said: 'This is the task which your king,
whoever he is who commands your ship, must complete
     for me;   230
after that he may take away the imperishable coverlet,
the fleece which glistens with its fringe of gold.'

So he spoke. Jason threw off his saffron cloak and, trusting
     in the god,
set his hand to the task. By the commands of the
     foreign woman,
skilled in all drugs, the fire did not cause him to flinch.
Drawing up the plough he forcibly bound the harness on
     to the bulls' necks,
and driving the relentless goad into their huge and
     powerful sides,
this powerful man completed his allotted task.
Aeetes let out a cry, albeit of wordless anguish, amazed at
     the man's strength.
Meanwhile his companions were holding out their hands to
     the mighty man,
and crowning him with wreaths of grass,   240
congratulating him with honey-sweet words.

Then the marvellous son of Helios* told him
where Phrixus' knives* had staked out the shining fleece;
but he did not expect him to accomplish that labour too,
for it lay in a coppice close to the ravening jaws of a serpent,
which in thickness and strength was bigger
than a fifty-oared ship, built by blows of iron tools.

But it is too far for me to travel by the high road, for
time presses.
I know a short way, on which I lead many others in poetic skill.

Arcesilas, by guile he killed the grey-eyed serpent with its
mottled back,   250
and with her willing help stole Medea away, who would
kill Pelias.
They reached the broad stretch of Ocean, the Red Sea,
and the country of the man-slaying Lemnian women;
there in athletic contests they competed with limbs' strength
for the prize of a garment, and slept with the women.
It was then, in foreign furrows, that the destined days or
nights
received the seed of your family's bright prosperity,
for there the race of Euphamus was sown and has endured
ever since.
They made their homes among men of Lacedaemon,
and in later time settled on the island of Calliste;*
from there Leto's son gave you the plain of Libya
to make it fruitful through the favour of the gods,   260
and to govern the divine city of golden-throned Cyrene,
since you have discovered the discretion that comes from
right judgement.

Learn now the wisdom of Oedipus:* if a man with a
sharp blade
lops off a shoot from a great oak and disfigures its
glorious form,
even though it can no longer bear leaves it casts a vote in its
own favour,
whether it comes at the end to a fire in winter
or, sustained by upright pillars in a master's house,

it performs a cheerless labour in an alien building,
having abandoned its native place.

You are a most timely healer, and Paean* honours your
    power to save.   270
To treat a festering wound you must apply a gentle hand;
it is easy, even for weaklings, to throw a city into convulsion,
but to establish it again in its place is hard indeed,
unless a god suddenly appears to steer its leaders.
For you, the pleasure that comes from doing this
is now being woven into a fabric. Be patient,
and devote your whole energy to serving prosperous Cyrene.
And among Homer's sayings* take this to heart and cherish it:
he said that in all affairs a good messenger brings the greatest
    honour;
even the Muse is exalted by a truthful report.

Cyrene and the distinguished house of Battus   280
have come to know the good sense of Damophilus:
he is young among the young, but in deliberations
he is an old man who has seen a hundred years;
he robs the wicked tongue of its clamorous voice,
and has learned to hate the arrogant,
but he does not fight against the good,
nor yet delays the fulfilment of any undertaking,
for opportunity's moment lasts but a short space for men.
He knows this well, and serves it as a steward, not as a
    hired man.
The cruellest thing, they say, is to know the good
but to be forced to stand apart from it.
And in truth he, like Atlas, now struggles under the weight
    of heaven,
far from his own land and possessions;   290
and yet immortal Zeus set the Titans free again.
In time, the wind dies down and sails are set again.
He prays that now he has drained his malignant sickness
to the dregs he may one day see his home,
and may at Apollo's spring* join in symposia
and many times pledge his heart to the pleasures of youth,
and in the company of discerning citizens

may hold the decorated lyre in his hands and attain peace,
causing no harm to anyone nor suffering it himself
at the hands of his fellow citizens.
Then, Arcesilas, he could tell what a spring of immortal verse
he found when he was recently a guest in Thebes.*

PYTHIAN 5

For Arcesilas of Cyrene, winner of the chariot race

Wide is the strength of wealth, when a mortal man receives it
from destiny's hand and, joining it with unsullied excellence,
takes it as an attendant who brings him many friends.
O Arcesilas, favoured by the gods, you have surely been
   searching for this,
along with glory, from the first steps of your brilliant life,
through the goodwill of Castor* of the golden chariot,
who after winter's rain* spreads a bright calm over your
   blessed hearth.   10

In truth, the wise handle power in a more noble fashion,
even when it is given by a god. And so with you,
as you walk the way of justice, great prosperity surrounds you;
first, because you are a king, and the inherited prestige
of great cities brings with it this most revered dignity,
when it is allied to judgement;*
and then, you are now blessed because you have won glory   20
at the famous Pythian games in the chariot race
and so have received this celebratory revel of men,
which brings delight to Apollo. Do not then forget,
as your praise is sung in Aphrodite's pleasant garden at Cyrene,
to attribute all your success to the god,
and also to hold Carrhotus* dear above all your companions.
When he returned to the palace of the Battidae, just rulers,
he did not bring with him Excuse the daughter of Hindsight,*
but after being entertained beside Castalia's waters   30
he crowned your head with the victorious chariot's prize,
won with reins unimpaired through the twelve swift laps
   of the sacred course.
For he shattered none of his strong equipment,
and now all that intricate work of skilled craftsmen
which he drove when he crossed the ridge of Crisa,*
on his way to the god's deep valley, is hung up in dedication.
A chamber of cypress wood encloses it, near the statue,*   40

cut in one piece from the living wood,
which bow-wielding Cretans set up in the temple on
    Parnassus.
It is therefore proper to greet one's benefactor with enthusiasm.

And on you, son of Alexibias, the fair-haired Graces have
    shed brightness.
You are blessed, in that after great exertion you have
    a memorial
of mighty words of praise: forty charioteers fell* but you
    kept your chariot intact   50
with fearless spirit, and have now returned from the
    glorious games
to the plain of Libya and your ancestral city.

No one is without his allotted share of toil, nor will be.
Yet the age-old prosperity of Battus persists,
though the fortune it confers varies this way and that;
it is a strong tower for the city, and for strangers a bright
    splendour.
Even deep-roaring lions* fled from him in fear
when he addressed them in his curious speech;
Apollo the colony's founder filled the beasts with sheer terror,   60
so that the oracles* he gave to Cyrene's steward should not
    be unfulfilled.

Apollo it is who dispenses cures for painful diseases to men
    and women;
he has also given them the lyre, granting the Muse to
    whoever he wishes,
instilling peace and good order in their hearts.
He is present in the secret places of his oracle, from where
    he caused
the mighty sons of Heracles and of Aegimius*
to settle in Lacedaemon and Argos and holy Pylos.   70
He makes known that my cherished glory is from Sparta,
whence sprang the Aegidae, my ancestors, who came to Thera—
not without the gods' favour, but some Fate led them.
From there we have inherited a communal meal of many
    sacrifices,

your Carneia, Apollo; and at your feast we honour*
    Cyrene's well-built city.   80
Here live the Trojans who delight in bronze weapons,
the sons of Antenor,* for they came here with Helen*
after they had witnessed their own land swathed in the
    smoke of war.
And that chariot-driving people is duly welcomed with
    sacrifices
and hailed with gifts by those whom Aristoteles* brought
    in swift ships,
opening up a deep path through the salt sea.
He planted larger sacred groves for the gods,
and laid down a straight broad way, to be a paved road,   90
sounding to the hammer of horses' hoofs
at processions in honour of Apollo, who brings help to mortals.
There, at the far end of the marketplace, he lies apart in death:
blessed when he lived among men,
and thereafter revered by the people as a hero.*
Separate from him before the palace lie the other holy kings
whose destiny places them in Hades. It may be that in
    their minds
below the earth they can hear of these great deeds of prowess,
sprinkled with soft dew and accompanied by waves of
    revel song,
                                   100
bringing them happiness for themselves
and a just share with their son Arcesilas in his distinction.

It is right for him to invoke Phoebus of the golden sword
in songs of young men, since he has been repaid from Pytho
by this elegant victory song for his expenditure.
The discriminating commend him, and I shall repeat what
    men say:
he cultivates a mind and eloquence beyond his years,   110
and in boldness he is a long-winged eagle among other birds.
In competition he has the strength of a tower,
in the Muses' company he takes wing, through his dear mother,
and he has proved himself a skilled charioteer.
He has walked with boldness along every road
which could bring his people renown, and now a god

has generously brought his power to fruition.
And so in time to come, you blessed children of Cronus,
allow him to possess an equal eminence in word and counsel,
that no stormy blasts of autumn winds* may disrupt his life
    to come.   120
In truth, the mighty mind of Zeus governs the destiny of men
    he loves;
I pray that he may award this prize to Battus' race, at Olympia.

PYTHIAN 6

For Xenocrates of Acragas, winner of the chariot race

Listen; for again we plough the field of glancing-eyed
    Aphrodite,
or of the Graces,* as we make our way to the temple
which is the navel-stone of the deep-roaring earth,
where in preparation for the wealthy Emmenidae,
for Acragas on its river, and indeed for Xenocrates,
a Pythian victor's treasure house of hymns has been erected
in the valley of Apollo, rich in gold;
which neither winter storm, summoned from
    loud-roaring clouds   10
like the onslaught of a pitiless army, nor wind
will carry away into the hidden places of the sea,
battered by the irresistible shingle,
but in a pure light its frontage shall bring to your father,
Thrasybulus, to be shared by your family, the news
of a chariot victory celebrated in the words of men
and won in the dales of Crisa.

In truth, by keeping it at your right hand,
you maintain the force of the principle   20
which they say Philyra's son* once in the mountains
commended to the mighty son of Peleus, left alone in his care:
above all gods to revere the son of Cronus,
the deep-voiced lord of thunder and lightning,
and never to withhold the same honour from his parents
during their destined span of life.

In former times, too, this thought was held by mighty
    Antilochus,
who stood firm against murderous Memnon, the Ethiopians'
    captain,
and died to save his father; for Nestor's chariot was encumbered   30
when his horse was wounded by Paris' arrows.
He was shaking his mighty spear,*
and the old Messenian's mind was confused;

he called out to his son, nor were his words flung idly to the
  ground.
That godlike man stood firm just where he was,
and bought his father's deliverance with his death,
and was considered by young men of that former generation   40
because of this stupendous deed to be unsurpassed
in dutiful behaviour towards his parents.

These things belong to the past; but among men of today
Thrasybulus comes nearest to the pattern of filial devotion,
and runs his uncle close in every kind of splendid display.
He is wise in handling his wealth, and does not cull the flower
  of youth
with injustice or insolent excess, but chooses wisdom
in the secret garden of the Pierian Muses.
It is to you, Earthshaker, lord of the racing of horses,   50
that he attaches himself, and his thoughts delight you greatly;
and among his companions in the symposium
his sweet spirit exceeds the honeycombed labour of bees.

PYTHIAN 7

For Megacles of Athens, winner of the chariot race

Athens, that great city, is the finest prelude to lay down
as a foundation for songs in praise of a chariot victory
won by the powerful Alcmaeonidae.
Could you make your home in a land
whose name enjoys a more glorious fame in Hellas?
No, for the tale of Erechtheus'* citizens is known in
    every city,
they who have made your temple at holy Pytho, Apollo,   10
a marvellous sight. Five victories at the Isthmus drive me on,
and one glorious triumph at Zeus' Olympian festival,
and two at Cirrha, Megacles, won by your clan and its
    ancestors.
I am pleased at your recent good fortune,
but grieved that success is repaid with envy.
Yet this, they say, is how the world goes: 20
happiness that thrives and stays with a man
brings with it now good things, now bad.

PYTHIAN 8

For Aristomenes of Aegina, winner in the wrestling

Benevolent Concord, daughter of Justice, who makes cities great,
holder of the paramount keys of counsel and war,
accept this hymn in honour of Aristomenes, victor at Pythia.
For you know how to practise gentleness and how to receive it,
unerringly choosing the right moment for each.
But when a man drives pitiless anger into his heart
you roughly confront your enemy's strength,   10
and sweep his insolent violence into the bilges.
Not even Porphyrion* was aware of your nature
when he presumptuously provoked you.
Gain is most prized when one has it from the house of a
    willing donor,
but violence overthrows a man in the end, however loud
    his boasts.

Typhos* the hundred-headed Cilician could not escape this fate,
nor indeed could the king of the Giants,
but they were beaten down by the thunderbolt and Apollo's
    arrows,
who with kind intent welcomed Xenarces' son* home from
    Cirrha,
crowned with Parnassian wreaths and Dorian victory revel.   20

Nor did this just island city fall far from the Graces,
sharing as it does in the glorious achievements of the Aeacids.
From the beginning it has enjoyed matchless fame,
for it is celebrated in song for its nurture of heroes, pre-eminent
in many victorious games and in the mêlée of battles,
and moreover is renowned for its citizens.

But I have no leisure to commit a full and lengthy account   30
to the lyre and to the soft-toned voice,
for that way an irksome surfeit may intervene.
Rather let what lies at my feet, the urgent debt I owe you,
    my boy—

your latest glorious success—take wings by means of my art.
For in following the trail of your mother's brothers
as a wrestler you do not shame Theognetus* at Olympia
or brawny Cleitomachus, victor at the Isthmus;
but in glorifying the family of Meidylidae
you bear out the words which Oecles' son* once spoke in riddles
as he saw the sons at seven-gated Thebes standing fast
    with their spears,   40
when the Epigoni had come from Argos on their second
    expedition.
As they fought he spoke:
'The fathers' noble spirit is plain to see, fixed by nature in
    their sons:
I can clearly make out the speckled snake on Alcman's
    flashing shield
as he brandishes it in the forefront by Cadmus' gates;
and he who suffered in a former disaster, the hero Adrastus,
now encounters news of a better omen,   50
though in his own home his fortune will be reversed:
for alone of the Danaan army he will gather up his dead
    son's bones,
but, by the will of the gods, will return
to the wide streets of Abas* with his company unharmed.'

So spoke Amphiaraus; and I too am glad to throw garlands
    at Alcman
and to rain hymns upon him, because he is my neighbour
and guardian of my wealth, and came to meet me
on my way to the navel-stone of the earth, celebrated in song,
and made use of his prophetic hereditary skills.*   60

And you, Far-shooter,* who rule over your famous temple
in the dales of Pytho where all are welcomed,
it was there you granted him the greatest source of joy;
and formerly at his home, at your joint festival,
you brought him the longed-for gift of the pentathlon.*
Lord, I pray that you will with favourable mind
and in a spirit of amity look upon every step of my journey.
Next to the sweetly singing revel band Justice has taken
    her stand;   70

I ask, Xenarces, that the gods' favour may be without envy
towards your family's fortunes;
for if someone achieves great things without long toil
he seems to many to be a wise man among fools,
equipping his life with judicious strategies.
But these things do not lie with men; it is god who provides.
Now raising one man high, now thrusting another down
    under his hands,
he goes down into the arena with an even hand.

Aristomenes, you won the prize at Megara and in
    Marathon's valley,
and were three times victorious by your exertions at
    Hera's local games.   80
On four bodies you sprang from above with hurt in mind;
for them no homeward way was decreed at the Pythia happy
    as yours,*
nor did welcome laughter give rise to encompassing joy
when they returned to their mothers, but, shunning their
    enemies
they slink home down alleyways, gnawed by failure.
But the man to whom fate has granted some recent success
flies up in great splendour on the wings of deeds of manly
    prowess,   90
and his concerns are with more than riches.
Men's pleasure swells in a brief space of time,
and likewise falls to the ground, shaken by an adverse judgement.

Creatures of a day! What is man? What is he not?
He is the dream of a shadow; yet when Zeus-sent
    brightness comes
a brilliant light shines upon mankind and their life is serene.

Aegina, dear mother, protect this city on its freeborn voyage,
aided by Zeus, king Aeacus, Peleus, noble Telamon
    and Achilles.*   100

PYTHIAN 9

For Telesicrates of Cyrene, winner of the race in armour

I proclaim, with the help of the deep-girdled Graces,
a victory of Telesicrates in the bronze shield race at Pytho;
I wish to shout aloud his good fortune,
and how he has crowned horse-driving Cyrene,
whom the flowing-haired son of Leto* once carried off
from Pelion's* echoing windy valleys
and bore the virgin huntress away in a golden chariot
to a place where he made her mistress of a land
teeming with flocks and superabundant in fruits,
to live in the beautiful and prosperous third root* of
   the mainland.

Silver-footed Aphrodite lightly touched his god-built chariot
with her hand and welcomed her Delian guest,   10
and over the pleasures of their marriage-bed she cast
   beguiling modesty,
linking in close harmonious union the god
and the daughter of wide-ruling Hypseus,
who at that time was king of the haughty Lapiths,*
a hero in the second generation from Oceanus;
the Naiad Creusa, daughter of Earth, had given him birth
in Pindus' famous dales, after enjoying the pleasure
   of Peneus' bed.
He raised his daughter, fair-armed Cyrene;
but she had no interest in walking to and fro before the loom,
or in the delights of feasts at home with girl companions,
but with bronze spears and sword she fought and killed
   wild beasts
and indeed brought great peace and security to her   20
   father's cattle,
spending but a short time with her sweet bedfellow,
sleep, that would drop on her eyelids just before dawn.

Once the far-shooter Apollo, lord of the wide quiver, found her
struggling alone, unarmed, with a huge lion.

Quickly he summoned Chiron from his home, and said:
'Son of Philyra, leave your holy cave and wonder   30
at this woman's spirit and mighty power;
see how she conducts her fight with unfaltering resolution,
a girl with a heart that rises above hardship
and a spirit that is untouched by storms of fear.
What man fathered her? From what stock has she been
    torn away,
living in these shadowy mountains' hidden places,
and making trial of her boundless strength?
Is it permitted to lay my illustrious hand on her
and reap the honey-sweet flower of her bed?'

The mighty centaur smiled subduedly, with an indulgent
    lift of his brow,
and at once spoke and gave him his advice:
'Secret are the keys to divine acts of love which are held by
    wise Persuasion,
Phoebus, and men and gods alike hold back   40
from taking the first open step towards the joys of
    sweet congress.
And so it is with you: it is not lawful for you to touch untruth
but your tender feelings have led you astray,
so that you dissemble in your words.
Do you ask this girl's ancestry, lord, you who know
the ordained end of everything, and all the paths that
    lead thereto?
How many leaves the earth sends forth in spring,
how many grains of sand in sea and river are churned up
by blasts of waves and winds; what will come to pass,
and whence it will come—all this you know well.
But if I must really pit myself against a wise god, I shall speak.   50

'It is as this girl's husband that you have come to this dale,
and you are destined to carry her over the sea to Zeus'
    magnificent garden,*
where you will make her ruler of a city, after assembling
an island people* on a hill in a plain. Even now queenly Libya
of the broad meadows is ready to welcome your glorious bride
with gladness in her golden palace, where she will without delay

bestow on her a portion of land to possess by right,
with its full share of all kinds of fruits, and not unknown
    to wild beasts.
There she will bear a son, whom renowned Hermes
will take from his dear mother and carry off
to Earth and to the Seasons on their fine thrones.   60
They will marvel at the child on their knees, and drip
    nectar and ambrosia
on to his lips, and make him immortal: a Zeus, or a holy Apollo,
a joy to men who revere him, a close companion of their flocks;
Agreus and Nomius* will be his name, though others will
    call him Aristaeus.'

So he spoke, and urged him to attain the sweet consummation
    of marriage.
When the gods are in haste fulfilment is swift and ways are short:
that same day saw the matter accomplished,
and they were united in the rich golden chamber of Libya,
where now she presides over a beautiful city, famous in
    the games.   70
And now at sacred Pytho the son of Carneiadas*
has linked her with flourishing good fortune;
his victory there has published Cyrene's fame,
and she will gladly welcome him to her land of beautiful women,
for he brings coveted glory back from Delphi.

Great prowess always brings forth many words,
but when the list is long discriminating people
prefer to hear a few themes amplified;
appropriateness in all things equally is the best.

Long ago seven-gated Thebes knew that Iolaus* too
    endorsed this dictum: 80
when he had struck off Eurystheus' head with his sword's edge
they buried him in the earth below in the tomb where his
    grandfather lay,
Amphitryon the charioteer, who was the guest-friend of the
    Sown Men
after he had left home for the streets of the Cadmeans, home
    of white horses.

Wise Alcmene lay with him and with Zeus,
and in a single labour bore mighty twin sons, victorious in battle.
Dull is the man whose speech cannot encompass Heracles,
or who is for ever unmindful of the waters of Dirce*
which fed both him and Iphicles. For them I shall sing
   this praise
because of the good fortune I enjoyed in answer to my prayer.
May the pure light of the loud-voiced Graces not desert me,   90
for at both Aegina and, yes, three times on the hill of
   Nisus*
he, I say, has glorified this city, by his efforts evading impotent silence.
So let no citizen, friend or foe, conceal this labour for the
   common good,
and so treat with contempt that saying of the Old Man of
   the Sea:*
'Give even to your enemy unfeigned and due praise, if he has
   done well.'
Telesicrates, when they saw you win so often at Pallas' annual
   festival,
and at Olympian games and at those of deep-bosomed Earth,*
and in every contest in your own country, each girl would
   wish in silence
that it was you who were her dearest husband, or son.   100

As for me, while I may quench the thirst for songs,
someone demands payment of a debt: that I should call up again
the ancient fame of his ancestors, as they were when they
   came to the city of Irasa*
for the sake of a Libyan woman, as suitors for the far-famed,
   fair-haired
daughter of Antaeus,* whom many of her noble kinsmen sought,
and many strangers too; for her beauty was marvellous,
and they wished to cull the blossoming fruit of her
   gold-crowned youth.   110

But her father was planning a more splendid marriage for his
   daughter.
He had heard how once at Argos Danaus* had found a way
to contrive the speediest of weddings for his forty-eight
   unwed girls,

before midday: without delay he placed the whole group
at the course's end, and ordered them to decide by a foot race
which girl each of the heroes who had come to woo them
    should win.
In just this way did the Libyan offer his daughter, matching her
    to a bridegroom.
He dressed her in finery and set her by the finishing line as the
    ultimate prize,
and proclaimed to all that the man who ran in first
and touched her robes should be the one to carry her away.   120
Then Alexidamus, running clear in the swift race, took the noble
    girl by the hand
and led her through the mass of nomad horsemen.
Many were the leaves and crowns they rained on him,
and many the winged victory wreaths he had won before.

PYTHIAN 10

For Hippocleas of Thessaly, winner of the boys' long sprint race

Happy is Lacedaemon, blessed is Thessaly!*
Their kings both descend from one father, Heracles, supreme
    in battle.
Why do I make this assertion? Do I miss the mark?
No, because Pytho and Pelinna* and the sons of Aleuas
    command me,
wishing to bring to Hippocleas the fine voices of men singing
    in praise;
for he tastes success in the games,
and Parnassus' vale has declared him to the surrounding people
to be supreme among boys who ran the double race.

Apollo, sweet is the end for men, and the beginning brings
    success   10
when a god speeds it on. It must be by your devising
that Hippocleas has succeeded in this; but it is also by his
    inborn qualities
that he has walked in the footsteps of his father,
who was twice a winner at Olympia in the armour of Ares*
that withstands the jolts of war; and Phricias* was victorious too
in the contest in the deep meadow below Cirrha's crags.
May destiny continue to accompany them in the days to come,
and cause their proud wealth to bloom.
Now they have been allotted no small share in the good
    things of Hellas   20
may they meet no envious change of fortune from the gods.
The heart of a god may be untouched by pain,
but that man is happy and fit to be hymned by poets in song
who is victorious by the excellence of his hands or feet
and who wins the greatest prizes through daring and strength,
and in his lifetime has seen his young son duly gain a
    Pythian crown.
He will never climb the brazen heaven,
but of all the glories which our mortal race may reach

his voyage takes him to the farthest region.

But neither on foot nor by sea could you discover
the fabulous way to the gathering of the Hyperboreans.*   30
Perseus, leader of men, once entered their houses
and feasted with them, after he had come upon them
as they were sacrificing splendid hecatombs of asses to the god;
Apollo always takes special delight in their feasts and worship,
and laughs to see the beasts' upright arrogance.*
Nor is the Muse a stranger to their customs: everywhere
maidens whirl in the dance to the loud lyre and the pipes'
     strident voice.

At their merry feasts they bind golden laurel in their hair;   40
disease has no place among that holy people, nor ruinous
     old age,
but they live without toil or battle, avoiding Nemesis' severe
     judgement.
To the company of these blessed men Danae's son* once came,
guided by Athena; his heart exhaled boldness, and he killed
     the Gorgon
and carried off her head adorned with snaky hair
and brought to the island people a stony death.
To me, no marvel ever seems beyond belief, if the gods
     accomplish it.   50

Ease the oar, quickly drop the anchor from the prow
and drive it into the ground to save us from the rocky reef,
for the best hymns of praise flit like bees from one theme
     to another.
I trust that when the people of Ephyra pour forth my sweet music
beside the Peneius* I shall with my songs make Hippocleas
even more admired for his crowns by both peers and elders,
and an object of desire for young unmarried girls.

Truly, desires for different things scratch at men's minds;   60
as for a man's ambitions, he would achieve them
if he should take the heart's desire that lies before him;
but there is no means of telling what another year may bring.

I place my confidence in Thorax' kindly hospitality,
who has busied himself on my behalf, and has yoked

this four-horsed chariot of the Pierian Muses,
as friend to friend and cheerful guide to guide.
Testing on a touchstone proves gold, and the same goes for an
    upright mind.
We shall also praise his noble brothers,
because they extol and glorify the state of the Thessalians.   70
The piloting of cities lies in good men's hands;
it is their valued inheritance.

For Thrasydaeus of Thebes, winner of the boys' short sprint race

Daughters of Cadmus—Semele, neighbour of Olympian
   goddesses,
and Ino Leucothea, sharing a home with the sea-Nereids—
come with the nobly born mother of Heracles
into Melia's* presence in the sanctuary of golden tripods,
the treasury which Loxias honoured above all others
and named the Ismenion,* the truth-speaking seat of prophets;
there, daughters of Harmonia, he now summons a local
   company of heroines,
inhabitants of that land, to assemble together,
so that at nightfall you may sing aloud of holy Themis*
and of Pytho and the straight-judging navel of the earth,   10
for the sake of seven-gated Thebes and the contest at Cirrha,
where Thrasydaeus distinguished his ancestral hearth
by casting on it a third crown as victor in the rich ploughlands
   of Pylades,
guest-friend of Laconian Orestes;* who, after his father's
   murder,
was secretly saved from the violent hands and pain-laden
   treachery
of Clytaemestra by his nurse Arsinoe, at the time when
with the grey bronze that pitiless woman despatched
   Cassandra,   20
daughter of Dardanian Priam, to Acheron's* shadowy shore,
accompanied by the spirit of Agamemnon.

Was it the ritual killing of Iphigeneia at Euripus,* far from
   her homeland,
that stung her to summon the anger leading to this dreadful act?
Or was she enslaved by another's bed, seduced by nocturnal
   couplings—
a most abominable crime in young wives,
and one impossible to hide because of other people's tongues,
for fellow citizens are given to spreading scandal.

Prosperity contains in it an equal measure of envy,
while the grumbling of those who live a lowly life goes unheard.   30

The hero son of Atreus was himself killed
when he returned at last to famous Amyclae,
and he also caused the death of the maiden prophetess,
after he had burnt the Trojans' palaces, for the sake
     of Helen,
and had put an end to their sumptuous living.
His young son escaped to the old man Strophius,
a guest-friend who lived at the foot of Parnassus;
but in time, with the help of Ares, he killed his mother
and struck Aegisthus down in a pool of blood.

My friends,* though I followed a straight path at first
I have become bewildered at the place where the road forks;
or did some wind blow me off my course, like a boat at sea?   40
Muse, it is your task, since you have agreed to hire out your
     voice for silver,
to shift it this way and that—either to his father Pythonicus now
or to Thrasydaeus, since their happiness and glory are
     blazing forth.
In time past not only were they victors with their chariots,
and at Olympia captured swift brightness with their horses
in the famous games, but now at Pytho going down into
the naked stadion race they have confounded all Hellas by
     their speed.   50

May I desire good things from the gods,
striving only for what is within reach at my time of life.
In the city's affairs I find that the middle course
brings by far the most thriving prosperity,
and I condemn the state of a tyrant.
I strive for successes that serve the common good,
for thus the envious are kept at bay.
But if a man has attained the heights,
conducting himself in peace and avoiding terrible arrogance,
he may reach a better destination in dark death
because he has left to his beloved descendants
the best of all possessions—the fame of a good reputation.

This it is which marks out Iolaus son of Iphicles   60
as a theme for hymns, and powerful Castor, and you,
   lord Polydeuces*
—sons of gods, living one day in your homes in Therapne
   and the next on Olympus.

PYTHIAN 12

For Midas of Acragas, winner in the pipe-playing

Most beautiful and radiant of mortals' cities,
home of Persephone; you I pray to, who make your home on
a strongly built hill above the banks of Acragas,* nurse of sheep;
be gracious, O queen, and with the favour of gods and men
accept both this crown won at Pytho by honoured Midas,
and the man himself, who overcame all Hellas
in the art once invented by Pallas Athena,
when she wove music from the savage Gorgons' deadly dirge,
which she heard pouring forth from the unapproachable
    snaky heads
of the maidens in their painful struggle,   10
at the time when Perseus* with an exultant cry
carried off one of the three sisters,*
bringing death to the island of Seriphus* and its people.
He had indeed sapped the strength of Phorcus' outlandish
    offspring,
and, by despoiling fair-cheeked Medusa of her head,
had made Polydectes* regret his feast,
and the binding enslavement of his mother,* forced into
    his bed—
he was Danae's son, conceived, as our tale goes, from a liquid
    stream of gold.*
But when the virgin goddess had saved her favourite from
    these trials
she devised the complex music of the pipes,
to imitate with instruments the piercing lament
which was wrung from Euryale's grinding jaws.   20
A goddess invented it, but gave her invention to mortals
    to possess,
and called it 'the melody of many heads'.
Now it famously woos men to congregate at the games,
as often as it passes through thin-beaten bronze and the reeds,
trusty witnesses of the dancers, that grow in Cephisis' precinct
beside the city of the Graces* of beautiful dancing places.

If there is any happiness among men, it does not come without
    exertion.
Perhaps a god will bring it about today—for we cannot escape
    what is fated—
        30
but there will come a time which will strike a man unawares,
and give him one thing when he does not expect it, and hold
    another back.

NEMEANS

NEMEAN 1

For Chromius of Aetna, winner of the chariot race

Ortygia,* resting-place of Alpheus, offshoot of famous Syracuse,
couch of Artemis* the sister of Delos,
from you a hymn of sweet words rises up to frame
great praise for storm-footed horses in honour of Zeus of Aetna.
The chariot of Chromius, and Nemea, prompt me
to yoke a song of praise to his victorious exploits.
The foundations were laid by the gods
through this man's divinely given talents;
but it is success that marks the peak of supreme glory,   10
and the Muse loves to commemorate great contests.

So scatter brilliance over the island
which Zeus lord of Olympus gave to Persephone,
and, his hair falling forward with his nod,
promised that he would raise up fertile Sicily
with its high and prosperous cities
to be pre-eminent on the plentiful earth.
And Cronus' son granted her a horseman people
in love with bronze-armoured war,
and no stranger to the golden leaves of Olympic olive.

I have grasped the occasion to treat of many themes,
and have not marred them with falsehoods.
I stand singing of noble deeds
at the outer gates of a hospitable man,   20
where an acceptable feast has been prepared for me;
and this house is not unacquainted with frequent guests
    from abroad.
It has fallen to him to use good men against disparagers
as water against smoke.
Different men have different skills; one ought to walk in
    straight ways

and in competition use inborn abilities.
For strength attains its end through action,
and understanding through the advice of those who have
the natural talent to foresee the future.
Son of Hagesidamus, it is in your nature to make use of both.   30

I do not long to possess great wealth, hidden away in a palace,
but to enjoy what I have and to be well regarded
for being of service to my friends;
for the hopes of much-labouring men are all alike.

And when, for my part, I speak of great pinnacles of
    achievement,
I am glad to hold close to the example of Heracles,
calling up the ancient tale:
how, when Zeus' son had emerged from his mother's womb
with his twin brother into the amazing brilliance of day,
escaping her birth-pangs, golden-throned Hera was not
    unaware of him
as he lay there in yellow swaddling clothes.
The queen of the gods, furious in her heart, forthwith
    dispatched snakes,   40
and they made straight through the open doors
for the wide inner part of his chamber,
impatient to envelop the infants in their darting jaws.
But Heracles raised his head upright and set about his
    first battle,
seizing the two snakes by the throat in his two irresistible hands,
strangling them. Time passed, and forced the breath from
    their dreadful bodies.
Unendurable fear struck the women who attended
Alcmene's bed—for she had leapt naked to her feet from
    her couch,   50
and yet was trying to drive off the monsters' assault.
Quickly the Cadmeian chieftains ran up in a body with
    bronze weapons,
and Amphitryon too arrived, transfixed with piercing pain,
swinging his unsheathed sword in his hand—
for anguish at home weighs heavily on all alike,
while the heart is easily untroubled by another's distress.

He stood there in amazement, at once agonizing and full of joy,
as he saw the singular spirit and power of his son—
for the immortal gods had contradicted the messengers' report.
He summoned Teiresias the trustworthy seer who lived nearby,   60
the eminent prophet of highest Zeus,
who made known to him and to all the people
what fortunes Heracles would meet,
how many beasts he would kill on land, and how many at sea,
all ignorant of justice. Further, he said that
he would cut down in a most horrible doom any man
who walked in the crooked way of excess;
for he foretold that when the gods would fight with the Giants
on the plain of Phlegra,* their bright hair would be soiled
    with earth
under a shower of his arrows; but that he himself
in uninterrupted peace for all time would receive   70
as his special portion relief from his labours
in a blessed palace; he would take Hebe as his fruitful wife,
and hold his wedding feast at the side of Zeus Cronus' son,
and sound the praises of his revered rule.

NEMEAN 2

For Timodemus of Acharnae, winner in the pancration

Even as the sons of Homer,* singers of stitched verses,
begin for the most part with a prelude to Zeus,
so has this man laid a first foundation of victory in the
    sacred games
at the much-hymned grove of Nemean Zeus.
And if indeed his life has guided him unerringly
on the road of his ancestors and given him as a glory to
    great Athens,
it must surely be that the son of Timonous
will often pluck the finest flower of prizes at the Isthmian games
and will also be victorious at the Pythian;
it is likely that Orion will closely follow the mountain-born
    Pleiades.*

10

And indeed Salamis is surely able to nurture a fighting man.
Ajax* at Troy had the better of Hector, and in the pancration
you, Timodemus, are exalted by your strength and perseverance.
Acharnae has long been famous for its noble men,
and in all matters of the games
the Timodemidae are acknowledged as supreme.
Four times they have carried off the prize
at the games under high-ruling Parnassus,
and in the valleys of excellent Pelops
have already donned eight crowns at the hands of the men
    of Corinth;*
seven at Nemea, in the games of Zeus,
and at home victories beyond number.
Citizens, include Zeus in your revel for Timodemus' brilliant
    homecoming,
and lead off with a voice of sweet melody.

20

NEMEAN 3

For Aristocleides of Aegina, winner in the pancration

Lady Muse, my mother, I pray you, come in this sacred
    Nemean month*
to the hospitable Dorian* island of Aegina,
for young men, artificers of honey-voiced revels,
impatient for your voice, await you by Asopus'* waters.
Each deed thirsts after something different,
but victory in the games loves song above all,
which is the deftest attendant of garlanded success.
Grant me, through my craft, an abundance of it.
You are Zeus' daughter:* begin a hymn   10
acceptable to the lord of the many-clouded sky,
and I shall pass it on to these voices and to the lyre.

It will be a pleasing labour to adorn this land,
where the Myrmidons* lived in former times,
whose famous meeting place Aristocleides has not sullied—
thanks to your favour—by acts of ignominy,
by growing soft in the pancration's strenuous tournament.
He has earned in his triumph a healing remedy
against the wearying blows endured on Nemea's low-lying plain.

If the son of Aristophanes, handsome as he is
and a doer of deeds which match his beauty,
has reached the ultimate in feats of manhood,   20
it is yet no easy matter to press on to the unsailed sea
beyond the pillars of Heracles,*
which the hero-god set as conspicuous witnesses
to the furthest limit of his seafaring.
He overcame monstrous creatures in the sea,
and alone explored channels through the shallows,
by which he reached the goal that returned him home,
and he mapped out the land.

My heart, to what foreign cape do you deflect my course?
It is to Aeacus and his family that I order you to carry the Muse.

The essence of justice keeps to this maxim, 'Praise what is noble.'
It is not best for a man to give in to yearnings for
      exotic themes;   30
seek nearer home, for you have been assigned fitting matter
to make into a sweet song of praise.
King Peleus delighted in his prowess in time past,
when he had cut his enormous spear—
he who captured Iolcus* alone, without an army,
and with a great struggle carried off the sea-nymph Thetis.*
Mighty Telamon* stood beside Iolaus and crushed Laomedon,
and with him once went after the powerful Amazons of the
      bronze bows,
and never did man-subduing fear hold back the edge of his
      resolution.

It is by inborn distinction that a man gains authority,   40
while he who has only been taught is a man of shadows;
he veers hither and thither, and never enters the arena with
      a confident step,
trying out thousands of exploits in his futile mind.

But fair-haired Achilles, when still a child in Philyra's* house,
did great deeds in play: poising his short iron spear in his hands,
swift as the winds, he would often spread carnage
while battling with wild lions, and would slaughter boars.
He would bring their gasping bodies to the centaur, Cronus' son,
first when he was six years old, and then for ever after.
Artemis was amazed, and intrepid Athene too,   50
at his killing of deer without dogs and cunning nets,
for he ran them down on foot.
I have the tale from men of former times
that deeply wise Chiron raised Jason in his stone habitation,
and after him Asclepius, whom he taught the soft-handed craft
      of medicine.
Later he arranged the marriage of Nereus' beautiful daughter,
and reared her mighty offspring,
building his spirit up in all appropriate ways,
so that when he was driven by gusting sea winds to fight
      before Troy
he would be able to withstand the spear-clattering battle-cry   60

of Lycians and Phrygians and Dardanians,*
and, when he came to grips with the spear-bearing Ethiopians,
would set the purpose firmly in his heart that their
    king Memnon,*
Helenus' fiery cousin, should not return home again.

From his deeds beams steadily the far-shining light of
    Aeacus' clan,
for yours is the blood, Zeus, and yours the games
which my hymn strikes upon, chanting this land's delight
in the voices of its young men.
Victorious Aristocleides merits the loud song,
for he has tied this island to splendid renown,
and Apollo's solemn Thearion* with glorious ambition.   70
It is in the trial that a man shows clearly how he will emerge
    superior:
as a boy among boys, as a man among men,
and thirdly among the old; thus do we mortal men live each
    portion of life.
There are moreover four virtues* that our human existence drives
    us towards,
and instructs us to consider what lies before us.
In these you* are not deficient; good health, my friend!
I send you this honey blended with white milk, as you see,
crowned with stirred dew, a draught of song
attended by the breath of Aeolian* pipes, late* though it is.
The eagle is swift among birds, and swooping from afar   80
seizes in its claws its blood-spattered prey,
while chattering jackdaws keep to the lower air.
But for you now, through the favour of fair-throned Cleo,*
and by virtue of your spirit, avid for victory,
the light shines out from Nemea and Epidaurus and Megara.*

NEMEAN 4

For Timasarchus of Aegina, winner in the wrestling

Joy is the best healer after the judgement of the strenuous
    contest;
and songs, too, poetic daughters of the Muses, soothe the victor
with their touch. Nor does warm water ease his limbs
as much as praise, partner of the lyre.
Words live longer than deeds, words which the tongue,
with the Graces' favour, draws from the mind's depths.

May I compose such words as the revel prologue to my hymn,
for Cronus' son Zeus, for Nemea, for Timasarchus'
    wrestling skill;
and may they be welcomed in the strongly built house
    of the Aeacids,*
this guiding light of justice which welcomes every stranger!
If your father Timocritus were still warmed by the fierce sun
he would often have accompanied this song,
playing a complex melody on the lyre,
loudly celebrating the victory of his son
who has brought back a string of crowns from Cleonae's games*
and from illustrious shining Athens;
and because at seven-gated Thebes, beside Amphitryon's*
    splendid tomb,
the Cadmeians* gladly heaped flowers on him, out of regard
    for Aegina.
For, coming to his hosts' city as a friend to friends,
he looked across at the rich court of Heracles,
with whom mighty Telamon once devastated Troy*
and the Meropes and the terrible warrior Alcyoneus—*
but not before he wrecked twelve four-horsed chariots with
    a rock,
killing the horse-trainer heroes riding in them, two in each.
The inexperienced in warfare will clearly not understand
    this tale;
those who achieve must expect to suffer as well.

10

20

30

But custom and the hurrying hours preclude a lengthy account,
and my heart is drawn as if by the wryneck's spell*
to touch on the festival of the new moon.*
And yet, though the deep salt sea grips you by the waist,*
hold out against its scheming; we shall enter the contest
in full daylight, far stronger than our adversaries,
while another man, with envy in his eyes,
pours out his empty opinions in darkness,   40
and they fall to the ground.

As for me, whatever talents Lord Destiny has granted me,
I know that advancing time will surely bring them to fulfilment.
Weave then this song to its end without delay, sweet lyre,
in the Lydian mode,* one loved by Oenone* and Cyprus,
where Teucer son of Telamon* rules, far from home;
while Ajax holds Salamis,* his ancestral land,
and Achilles his bright island in the Euxine sea.*
Thetis rules in Phthia,* and Neoptolemus in the continuous
     mainland,   50
where lofty cattle-grazing ridges slope down from Dodona
to the Ionian sea.* At Pelion's foot Peleus* fell upon Iolcus
with warlike hand and handed it over in slavery to
     the Haemones,*
having suffered from the crooked wiles of Hippolyta, wife
     of Acastus.
Pelias' son had tried to kill him in ambush with the sword
     of Daedalus,*
but he was saved by Chiron, and so fulfilled the fate destined
     for him by Zeus: 60
he baulked the all-conquering fire, the knife-edged claws
     and terrible teeth
of boldly plotting lions, and married a high-throned Nereid.*
He saw the splendid circle of seats where the kings of heaven
     and earth sat
and revealed their gifts and the power which would come to
     his race.

But it is not permitted to pass to the west of Gadeira;*
set your ship's sails back to Europe's mainland,   70
for I cannot run through the whole tale of Aeacus' offspring.

My contract is with the Theandridae,* and I have come here to be
a prompt herald of limb-building contests at Olympia, at the
    Isthmus, and at Nemea.
After competing there they always return home with a glorious
    harvest of crowns—
where, Timasarchus, we hear that your family is an adherent of
    victory songs.
If indeed you command me to set up a pillar, whiter than Parian
    marble,
to your uncle Callicles—as refined gold reveals all its brilliance,   80
so a hymn to a man's brave deeds puts his fortune on a level
    with kings.
May he, in his home by Acheron, hear my voice
singing of the place where, at the deep-rumbling
    Trident-holder's games,*
he was crowned with Corinthian wild celery—
he of whom, my boy, your aged grandfather Euphanes once
    gladly sang.   90

Every generation is different, and each man expects
to claim as exceptional what he himself has witnessed.
So a poet might emulate Melesias* as he twisted in the contest,
weaving his phrases, not to be thrown in the argument's grapple,
treating the noble with gentle attention
but for the ill-willed a harsh opponent in the next round.

NEMEAN 5

For Pytheas of Aegina, winner in the youths' pancration

I am no sculptor, to create images which stand motionless on
    their base.
No, sweet song, you must go forth from Aegina on every ship
    and merchantman,
carrying the news that Lampon's powerful son Pytheas
has won the pancration crown at Nemea;
his cheeks do not yet show late summer, mother of the soft
    grape-bloom,
but he has brought honour to the Aeacids,*
warrior heroes born of Cronus and Zeus with the golden
    Nereids,
and to his mother-city, a land welcoming to strangers;
which once Endais' famous sons* and mighty lord Phocus   10
(he whom divine Psamatheia bore on the seashore),
standing beside the altar of father Hellenius*
and holding their hands wide up to the sky
prayed might be celebrated for its ships and as a home
    of brave men.

I shrink from telling of their grave deed, one ventured
    without justice,
how indeed they left the famous island
and what destiny drove these mighty men away from Oenone.
Here I shall stop; not every truth is the better for showing its
    real face,
and silence is often the wisest course for a man to devise.
But if it is wealth or strength of hands or iron war that is to
    be praised,
then let someone dig me a wide jumping-pit from this place,   20
for I have a nimble spring in my knees,
and eagles may soar beyond the sea.

For these people* too the Muses' beautiful chorus sang on Pelion,
and among them Apollo swept the seven-tongued lyre
with a golden plectrum, and led them in diverse melodies.

They began with Zeus, and first sang a hymn for revered Thetis
and for Peleus, telling how the alluring Hippolyta,*
    Cretheus' child,
desired to shackle him by guile, having persuaded her husband,
master of the Magnetes, by artful scheming to be her
    accomplice;
she fabricated a false, contrived story that he was attempting
to enjoy her as his wife in Acastus' marriage-bed.   30
But the opposite was the case: many times she had artfully
    begged him
with all her heart, but her vehement words only provoked
    his anger,
and he swiftly rebuffed the wife, fearing the rage of the Father,
patron of guests; and Zeus, cloud-summoning king of the
    immortals,
understood him well from heaven, and promised he would soon
have a sea-nymph, a Nereid of the golden distaff, to be his bride,
after he had won over her suitor Poseidon,* who often comes
    from Aegae*
to the glorious Dorian Isthmus, where joyful companies
welcome the god with the cry of the pipe,
and strive with each other in their limbs' confident strength.

Inborn Destiny determines the outcome of every deed.   40
Twice, Euthymenes, you came from Aegina,
and falling into Victory's arms were favoured with
    intricate hymns;
and even now, Pytheas, your mother's brother speeds
    behind you
and exalts the family he shares with that man.*
Nemea, and the month that Apollo loves,* is his true support;
he overcame his peers who came to meet him,
both at his home and in the lovely valleys of Nisus' hill.*
I rejoice that the whole city competes for honourable prizes.

Know that it was truly through the good fortune of
    Menander's* aid
that you won a sweet recompense for your labours.
It is just that a builder of athletes should hail from Athens;
but if it is of Themistius you have come to sing,   50

hesitate no longer, give voice, unfurl your sails at the
   highest yard,
and declare him boxer and pancratiast,
doubly distinguished by victory at Epidaurus.
Bring crowns of leaves and flowers to Aeacus' temple portico,*
in the company of the fair-haired Graces.

NEMEAN 6

For Alcimidas of Aegina, winner in the boys' wrestling

There is one race of men, and one of gods,
though from one mother we both draw our breath.
A division of power keeps us entirely separate:
the one is nothing, the other has an eternal home in the secure
    brazen heaven.
Even so, we resemble the immortals in some respects,
in greatness of mind or of stature,
though we do not know by day or night
what finishing line destiny has marked out for us to run towards.

And now Alcimidas gives us the proof to see
how inborn talents resemble crop-yielding fields,
which by turns yield men an abundant livelihood from
    the ground   10
and then again lie fallow and so gain strength.
Indeed, there has come from the lovely games at Nemea
a competitor who has followed this destiny fixed by Zeus
and now shows himself to be no portionless hunter at wrestling,
but setting his feet in the kindred tracks of his grandfather
    Praxidamas;*
for he was a victor at Olympia, the first to bring garlands back
from the Alpheus to the clan of Aeacus; five times crowned
    at the Isthmus
and three times at Nemea, he rescued Socleides* from
    obscurity,   20
so that he became the greatest of the sons of Hagesimachus—
for he had three prize-winning sons,
who tasted hardship and reached the peak of excellence.
Helped by the gods, their boxer's craft has shown us that no
    other house
is holder of more crowns, won at the very centre of Hellas.

I hope in this bold boast to hit the mark full on,
shooting like an archer from my bow.

Come, Muse, guide a glorious wind of poetry onto this house,
for when men die it is songs and stories that recall their
    fine deeds;   30
in these the Bassidae, a family famed of old, are not deficient
for their ships carry a cargo of their own praise,*
and by virtue of their noble achievements
they can give the Pierians' ploughmen* much matter for hymns.

So indeed one of the same bloodline, Callias,
once at holy Pytho bound his fists with thongs and was victorious,
pleasing the offspring of Leto* of the golden distaff,
and in the evening* by Castalia shone like a flame
in the Graces' clamorous company;
and the bridge of the tireless sea* honoured Creontidas
in Poseidon's precinct at the biennial bull-slaying festival   40
held by the people who live round about;
and once the lion's herb covered his victor's brow
underneath the ancient shady mountains of Phlius.*

Broad are the approach roads from every direction
for poets to celebrate this famous island,
for by the revelation of their great achievements
the Aeacids have granted it an outstanding destiny,
and their name wings far and wide over land and sea—
it leapt even to the Ethiopians when Memnon failed to return,   50
when Achilles* stepped from his chariot to the ground
and fell upon them, a heavy opponent,
on the day he slaughtered the shining dawn's son
at the point of his furious spear.

Poets of former times have discovered this high road,
and I myself follow them, intent on my theme.
But it is always the wave which rolls over the ship's rigging,
they say, that especially perturbs a man's heart;
I shoulder a double burden on my willing back
and come as a herald to declare that this is the twenty-fifth
    success
brought home from the games that men call sacred
which you, Alcimidas, have conferred on your famous clan—   60

though the lot that was drawn deprived you,* my boy, and
   Polytimidas
of two Olympian wreaths by the precinct of Cronus' son.
To a dolphin, swift through the salt sea, I would liken
Melesias, a charioteer of skill and strength.

NEMEAN 7

For Sogenes of Aegina, winner in the boys' pentathlon

Eleithyia, enthroned beside the deep-pondering Muses,
daughter of powerful Hera, bringer to birth of children—*
hear me; without you we cannot look upon the light or the
    dark night,
nor receive our portion of your sister, shining-limbed Hebe.
Yet we do not all draw breath with equal chances;
different things hold each man back, yoked to destiny.

But with your help Sogenes Thearion's son is sung to fame,
renowned for his prowess among pentathletes.
His home is the song-loving city of the spear-clashing Aeacids,
and they are well pleased to honour a spirit tested in
    competition.   10

If a man succeeds in any enterprise, he throws a honeyed theme
into the Muses' waters; for when they lack hymns
great feats of courage live in deep darkness.
We know of one way only to mirror fine deeds:
if, by the help of shining-capped Mnemosyne,*
some recompense for a man's toil is found in splendid
    poetic song.
Wise men* have learnt of the wind that comes on the third day,
and they are not corrupted by gain;
rich and poor alike must make their way to the tomb of death.   20

Odysseus' fame, I believe, is greater than his true experience
because of Homer's sweet poetry,
for there is a grandeur in his lies and soaring artifice,
and his poetic skill misleads and deceives us with its stories.
The mass of mankind is blind in heart;
if they had been able to discern the truth,
mighty Ajax* would not have driven his polished sword
into his breast, angered over the award of arms—
Ajax, Achilles apart, the strongest in battle of those
whom the escorting winds of straight-blowing Zephyrus

conveyed in swift ships to the city of Ilus*
to recover the wife of fair-haired Menelaus.   30
But the surge of Hades comes to all alike,
and falls on men whether they expect it or not.
Honour attends those whose story is enriched by a god
     after death;
as a helper he came* to the great navel of broad-bosomed earth.
In Pytho's earth lies Neoptolemus, when he had sacked
     Priam's city,
where the Danaans too had suffered,
but on his voyage home missed Scyros*
and, wandering with his crew, came to Ephyra.
In Molossia* for a short time he was king—
an honour his family has enjoyed for all time since;   40
but then he departed for the god,* bringing him wealth
from the finest of the spoils of Troy,
and there in a quarrel over sacrificial meat
a man whom he met stabbed him with a knife.*
His kindly Delphian hosts were greatly troubled;
but he had paid his debt to destiny,
for it was fated that one of the royal Aeacids
should abide for ever within the ancient grove
next to the well-built temple of the god,
and should live as a ritual overseer of the processions*
which honour heroes with numerous sacrifices.

To establish his just fame, three words will suffice:
it is no lying witness,* Aegina, that authenticates   50
the deeds of your and Zeus' offspring.
I feel the confidence to speak of a sovereign road of words,
reaching from your home, that honours your splendid
     achievements.
But respite is sweet in all undertakings, and even honey
and Aphrodite's flowers of pleasure can cause satiety.
Each one of us differs by nature in the life that is allotted him:
one man has this gift and another that, and it is impossible
for one person successfully to attain complete happiness.
I cannot speak of anyone to whom Destiny
has offered this as a secure and lasting gift.

To you, Thearion, she has given a fair share of prosperity;
you have acquired the boldness to do fine deeds,
and she does not harm your mind's intelligence.   60
I am your guest-friend; avoiding covert censure
I will honour the man who is my friend with genuine praise,
as if I were channelling water towards him,
for this is the fitting reward for good men.
No man of Achaea living above the Ionian sea
will approach me and take me to task;*
I trust in my friend's hospitality, and among his townsmen
my gaze is serene, since I do not exaggerate
and I thrust all violence from the path before my feet.
May the rest of my life steal up on me in kindliness;
any man of understanding will speak up
if I come here singing crooked lies out of tune.

Sogenes of the clan of the Euxenidae,   70
I swear I have not overstepped the mark
in launching my tongue swiftly like a bronze-cheeked javelin*
which exempts the strong neck from the sweat of the
     wrestling bout,
before the body is exposed to the blazing sun.
If there was toil, greater is the joy that follows it.
Let me be; if I was carried away and protested noisily,
I am not too uncouth to pay a victor his due.
Weaving crowns is an easy task—so strike up the prelude!
To be sure, the Muse binds gold and white ivory together
with the lily-like flower she steals from under the dew of
     the sea.*
Sing of Zeus, and rouse the far-famed voice of hymns   80
in honour of Nemea—but softly; it is fitting for us
to speak with a gentle voice of the king of gods in this place,
where men say he planted Aeacus* in the mother who took
     his seed,
to be a ruler in my famous land,* and, Heracles,
to be for you a kindly guest-friend and brother.

If a man takes delight in others' company, I would say that
a neighbour who loves him with steadfast intent
is a joy beyond all others. And if this holds true for a god as well,

Sogenes might with your help, Subduer of Giants,*
expect to live with good fortune, in tender duty to his father,
on the well-built sacred street of his ancestors;
for on both sides as he goes his house lies between your
        precincts,*
as if they were the yokes of four-horsed chariots.
O blessed one, it is right for you to win over Hera's husband
and his grey-eyed daughter,* for you can often give mortals
courage in the face of difficulties that are hard to surmount.
May you furnish him with a life of enduring strength,
and weave happiness into his youth to the end of shining
        old age,
and may his children's children ever enjoy this present honour   100
and even greater in time to come.
Never will my heart say* that it has carped at Neoptolemus
in unforgiving words; but to turn over the same ground
three or four times leads nowhere, just like one
barking at children, 'Corinth belongs to Zeus!'*

NEMEAN 8

For Deinias of Aegina, winner of the long sprint race

Lady Hora,* herald of Aphrodite's ambrosial tenderness,
who sits on the eyelids of young girls and boys,
you raise them up with the hands of necessity—
gentle for one, rough for another. In every undertaking
it is most desirable not to stray beyond just measure,
and to be able to secure loves of the nobler kind,
such as those, shepherds of the gifts of the Cyprian,*
which attended the bed of Zeus and Aegina.
From here a son was born, king of Oenone,*
supreme in action and counsel.
Many men many times begged to visit him,   10
for the flower of heroes from neighbouring lands
were ready and willing, unsummoned, to obey his rule;
both those who mustered their army in rocky Athens
and the descendants of Pelops in Sparta.

A suppliant, I clasp Aeacus' holy knees,
and on his dear city's behalf and these his citizens
I bring a Lydian headband patterned with resonant music,*
a Nemean decoration for the double stadion victories
of Deinias and of his father Megas.

In truth, if happiness is implanted by the gods
it endures longer among men, such as that
which freighted Cinyras* with wealth once in sea-girdled Cyprus.
Look, I stand here on poised feet,
catching my breath before I speak;*
many tales have been told, in many ways,   20
but to invent something new and test it on the touchstone,
that is absolute danger. To the envious, words are a tasty morsel,
and envy clutches at the noble, but picks no fight with
    inferior men.

This it was that glutted itself on Telamon's son,
making him fall hunched upon his sword—

indeed, many men of no eloquence but brave in heart
have been pinned down by oblivion, because of a harsh quarrel,
while the greatest glory is tendered to the slippery lie.
In a secret ballot the Danaans favoured Odysseus,
and Ajax, denied the golden armour, wrestled with a bloody death.*
Truly, the wounds were unequal which both had hacked
in their foes' warm flesh, as they toiled under cover of the
    protecting spear,   30
both over newly slain Achilles, and in other labours of
    death-dealing days.
Hateful slander indeed existed long ago as well,
accomplice of fawning tales, a cunning schemer,
mischief-working infamy, which crushes brilliance
but for obscure men raises up a festering glory.

Never may this temperament be mine, father Zeus,
but may I follow simple paths of life,
so that after my death I do not taint my children with ill repute.
Some men's prayers are for gold, others for limitless lands,
but mine are to please my fellow citizens,
and then to cover my limbs in earth,
having praised the praiseworthy and scattered reproof on the
    wicked.
Excellence soars upward like a tree fed on fresh dews,   40
lifted among the wise and just towards the liquid upper air.
The need for friends comes in many forms:
it is most valued in times of trouble,
but joy too craves to look upon trusty support.
O Megas, I cannot bring your life back again—
that is the futile desire of empty hopes—
but to set up a Muses' stone for your homeland and for the
    Chariadae,*
to celebrate your twice-famous feet, is an easy task.
I am glad to have broadcast a boast that fits your deeds,
for many a man has charmed the pain from toil   50
by chanting songs. Certainly the victory hymn existed long ago,
even before strife arose between Adrastus and the Cadmeans.*

NEMEAN 9

For Chromius of Aetna, winner of the chariot race

Let us go in revel company, Muses,
from Apollo's temple at Sicyon* to newly founded Aetna,
to Chromius' prosperous house,
where the wide-flung doors are overrun by guests.
Come, fashion a sweet hymn of verses,
for he mounts his chariot of conquering horses
and calls for an invocation to the mother and her twin children,*
who share the watch over sheer Pytho.

There is a saying among men, that a noble accomplishment
should not be hidden on the ground in silence;
what is needed is a divine song of heroic verse.
Let us then lift high the deep-voiced lyre
and lift up the pipe, for this very pinnacle of horse-races,
founded by Adrastus for Phoebus by the waters of Asopus.*
Mindful of this, I shall celebrate the hero   10
with honours that bring him renown.
He was king there at that time, and made his city great,
glorifying it with new festivals and trials of men's strength
and races with polished chariots.

Long before, he had fled bold-plotting Amphiaraus
and dreadful civil strife in his ancestral home in Argos;
for Talaus' sons,* forced out by faction, were no longer rulers there.
But the stronger man may bring past conflict to an end:
they gave the son of Oecles* man-slaying Eriphyle*
to be his wife, as a pledge of trust,
and he became the greatest of the fair-haired Danaans,
and in later time led an army of men to seven-gated Thebes
on a road that held no auspicious omens;
Cronus' son had shaken his lightning and exhorted them
not to set out from home with crazed intent,
but to abandon their expedition.   20

So the company, with bronze weapons and caparisoned horses,
pressed eagerly on, marching to certain ruin.

On the banks of Ismenus* they rejected a sweet return home,
fattening with their bodies the flowers of white smoke.
Seven pyres fed on the men's young limbs,
but for Amphiaraus Zeus with his all-powerful thunderbolt
split the earth's deep breast and buried him, horses and all,
before Periclymenus' spear could strike him in the back,
so bringing shame to the spirit of a fighting man;
for in god-sent panic even the sons of gods may flee.*

If it can be done, son of Cronus, I would hope to postpone
for as long as possible this proud trial of life and death
with the Phoenician army's spears; and I entreat you,
    Father Zeus,
to grant the children of Aetna's men a long and
    well-governed destiny,   30
and to gather their people together in public festivals.
For, as you know, they are lovers of horses there,
and men who keep their minds above possessions.

My words are difficult to believe, for love of gain
covertly steals away that sense of shame which brings renown.
But had you served as Chromius' shield-bearer
in the midst of foot-soldiers' and horsemen's shouts
or in battles at sea, you would have judged,
among the hazards of the shrill war-cry,
that in the conflict that goddess* was moving his warrior's spirit
to beat back the havoc of Enyalius.*
Few men can counsel how to turn with hand and spirit
the cloud of impending slaughter back on to their enemies' ranks.
It is said that Hector's glory burst into flower beside
    Scamander's stream;
but beside the steep rocky banks of Helorus,*   40
at the place which men call Areia's Crossing,
this same brightness shone on Hagesidamus' son in his
    early prime.
On other days I shall speak of his many feats,
some on the dusty land and others on the neighbouring sea.
After labours justly borne in youth life moves gently toward
    old age.
He should know that the gods have allotted him amazing happiness;

for if as well as his many riches a man earns the glory of fame,
there is no further mountain peak on which he may set his feet.

The symposium is the friend of peace, but newly won victory
also blossoms when attended by gentle song,
and the voice grows in confidence next to the mixing bowl.
Let someone stir it, the sweet inspirer of revelry,   50
and hand round the vine's potent child in the silver bowls*
which his mares once won for Chromius and sent to him
from holy Sicyon with ritually woven garlands of Leto's son.
Father Zeus, I pray that with the Graces' help
I may proclaim that success, and may outdo many men
in honouring his victory in my song,
throwing my javelin closest to the Muses' mark.

NEMEAN 10

For Theaeus of Argos, winner in the wrestling

Sing, Graces, of the city of Danaus* and his fifty daughters
on their bright thrones: Argos, Hera's home, fit for a goddess.
Its bold deeds cause it to blaze with countless exploits.
To tell of Perseus' encounter with the Gorgon Medusa*
would take too long, and many are the towns it founded
in Egypt as a result of the labours of Epaphus;*
nor did Hypermestra* wander from the path,
she who kept her one dissentient sword in its sheath.
Diomedes* long ago was made an immortal god
by the fair-haired goddess of the grey eyes;
and at Thebes the earth, smashed by Zeus' thunderbolts,
received and hid that storm-cloud of war,
the prophet son of Oecles.* From ancient times
Argos has excelled in its beautiful-haired women—   10
a reputation clearly proved by Zeus' advances to Alcmene*
    and Danae.*
In Adrastus' father* and in Lynceus* it blended
the fruit of intellect with straight-dealing justice.
It nurtured the spearman Amphitryon,* who in matchless
    good fortune
entered kinship with that god, when in his bronze armour
he killed the Teleboae; for, assuming his appearance,
the king of the immortals entered his hall,
carrying in him the fearless seed of Heracles,
whose wife Hebe,* most beautiful of goddesses,
paces Olympus beside her mother, presider over marriage.

My mouth is too small to tell of everything Argos' precinct holds
as its share of noble deeds; and men's satiety is hard to meet.   20
Even so, rouse the well-strung lyre and turn the mind
    to wrestling,
since the competition for bronze* urges the people
to go to Hera's ox-sacrifice and the judgement of the games,
where Oulias' son Theaeus was twice a victor

and found forgetfulness of the toils he so lightly endured.
At Pytho* too he once overcame a multitude of Hellenes,
and, travelling with good fortune, won crowns at Nemea and
  the Isthmus.
He gave the Muses employment for their plough,
by winning three times at the gates to the sea
and three times on sacred ground established by Adrastus.*

Father Zeus, his mouth is silent about his heart's true desires,*
for the fulfilment of all endeavours lies with you;
but when he prays for your favour he offers
daring and a heart not unfamiliar with labour.   30
I sing of matters known to the god,
and to all who struggle to reach the peaks of the paramount
  games.
Pisa mounts the highest event, instituted by Heracles,
but, by way of a prelude, sweet Athenian voices
have twice sung this man's praises at their rites,*
and to Hera's gallant people came the fruit of the olive
in richly patterned jars, earth baked by fire.

Theaeus, many times has honour from victory in the games
come to the famous family of your mother's forebears,
through the favour of the Graces and of the sons of Tyndareus.
If I were a kinsman of Thrasyclus or Antias*   40
I would not think it right to hide the light of my eyes in Argos.
How many times has this horse-rearing city of Proetus*
flourished because of victories in the valleys of Corinth!
Four times they came away rewarded by the men of Cleonae,*
and from Sicyon* laden with silver wine bowls,
and from Pellana* with soft woollen cloaks on their backs.
As for reckoning up their countless prizes of bronze,*
it is impossible, for I have too little time to calculate them—
prizes which Cleitor, Tegea, and the towering cities of Achaea
and Lycaeon offered beside the racecourse of Zeus,
to be won with the strength of hands and feet.

It is no wonder that they are natural athletes,*
for Castor and his brother Polydeuces came to Pamphaes' house   50
and were entertained; they who keep watch over spacious Sparta,

and share with Hermes* and Heracles the direction of
   successful games.
Deep is their regard for men of justice; the race of gods is
   indeed faithful.
Changing places turn by turn, they spend one day
with their dear father Zeus, and the next in earth's hidden places
in the hollows of Therapne,* fulfilling an equal destiny;
for when Castor died in battle Polydeuces chose this life
in preference to a wholly divine existence in heaven.

Idas, for some reason angered over cattle, had wounded Castor   60
with the point of his bronze spear; watching intently from
   Taygetus*
Lynceus,* who of all men had the keenest sight,
had seen them* sitting in an oak's hollow trunk.
On swift feet the sons of Aphareus at once ran up
and quickly plotted a prodigious deed,
and suffered terribly for it at the hands of Zeus;
for Leda's son* arrived in hot pursuit, while they stood their
   ground
next to their father's tomb, from which they had wrenched
Hades' marker of polished stone and hurled it at Polydeuces' chest,
but they could not crush him or force him backwards.
He leapt on them with his swift spear
and thrust the bronze into Lynceus' side.   70
Zeus flung at Idas a smoking fiery thunderbolt,
and they burnt together, all alone.
To encounter those who are stronger is a harsh struggle for men.
Quickly Tyndareus' son turned back to his mighty brother,
and found him not yet dead but shivering and gasping for breath.
Shedding hot tears, he groaned and cried aloud:
'Father, son of Cronus, what deliverance will there be from grief?
Pass sentence of death on me as well as on him, lord.
Honour vanishes when a man's friends are taken away,
and in times of suffering few mortals can be trusted to share
   his burden.'

So he spoke, and Zeus stood before him and uttered
   these words: 80
'You are my son; as for this man, your mother's hero husband

came to her after me and dropped his mortal seed in her.
But come, despite this I will grant you a choice:
you may wish to escape death and repellent old age,
and live with me on your own on Olympus,
together with Athene and Ares of the black spear,
and that will be your allotted destiny;
or, if you are your brother's champion and are minded
to share everything equally with him,
you may live half your life under the earth
and half in the golden palaces of heaven.'

So he spoke; and Polydeuces chose no wavering purpose in
   his heart,
but released* first the eye and then the voice of bronze-belted
   Castor.   90

NEMEAN 11

For Aristagoras of Tenedos, on being installed as a councillor

Hestia,* daughter of Rhea, by your allotted office
patron of council chambers, sister of Zeus on high
and Hera who shares his throne;
graciously welcome Aristagoras into your hall
next to your shining sceptre, and his companions
who honour you and keep Tenedos on an upright course,
venerating you as first among gods
often with libations and often with the savour of sacrifice.
For them the lyre and song fill the air,
and in their perpetual feasts the dictates of Zeus
Protector of Strangers are duly observed.

Grant that he* completes his twelve-month term   10
with distinction and with his heart unscarred.
I count his father Arcesilas* to be blessed,
in his physique that excites admiration,
and in his natural intrepidity.
If a man is rich and surpasses others in beauty,
and has given proof of his strength by victory in the games,
let him remember that his limbs' clothing is mortal,
and earth is the very last garment he will put on.

Yet he is justifiably praised in his citizens' generous words,
and we must fashion praise for him in honey-echoing songs.
Sixteen brilliant victories have crowned Aristagoras   20
and his illustrious family, won at regional games
in wrestling and the pancration, source of great pride.
His parents' diffident anxiety held their strong son back
from competing in the contests at Pytho and Olympia;
truly I swear that in my judgement
if he had gone to Castalia and Cronus' well-wooded hill*
he would have returned from the four-year festival
laid down by Heracles* more honoured than his adversaries,
revelling in his victory, his hair bound in bright crowns.

But empty-headed boasting hurls one mortal down from
   success,   30
and another, too little confident in his strength,
whose timid spirit drags him back by the hand,
falls short of the glory he deserves.

It was indeed easy to deduce that his* bloodline comes
   from Sparta,
from Peisandrus* long ago, who came with Orestes from
   Amyclae,
leading a bronze-armoured army of Aeolians to this place;
it is mingled with that of Melanippus, his mother's forebear,
who came from the waters of Ismenus.

Ancient qualities display their strength in alternate generations
   of men:
the dark ploughed earth does not yield a constant harvest,
nor, as the years wheel round, is it the rule
for trees to bear fragrant blossom of equal richness,   40
but they come and go. Just so destiny governs the mortal race;
no clear signal comes to mankind from Zeus.
For all that, we set sail with great ambitions
in our desire to do numerous deeds,
for our limbs are shackled by shameless hope,
and the streams of prescience lie far away.
In matters of gain, one should hunt out due measure;
the madness of inaccessible desires is too sharp to bear.

ISTHMIANS

ISTHMIAN 1

For Herodotus of Thebes, winner of the chariot race

Mother, Thebe* of the golden shield,
I shall judge your demands even above my want of leisure.
Let not rocky Delos,* whose concerns now absorb me,
be angry with me; for what is dearer to good men than
    cherished parents?
Give way, island of Apollo. With the gods' help
I shall complete both offerings of song together,
and celebrate in the dance both Phoebus of the unshorn hair
on sea-washed Ceos, with its seafaring men,
and also the sea-bounded ridge of the Isthmus,
since it has conferred on Cadmus' people* six crowns* from
    the games—
the honour of glorious victories for their country—
a land where also Alcmene bore her fearless son,*
before whom the dogs of Geryon once flinched in fear.

But it is for Herodotus that I fashion a gift of honour,
for his four-horsed chariot, and for his handling of its reins
with his own hands;* and I wish to associate him
with a hymn to Castor or to Iolaus,
for they were born to be the mightiest of hero charioteers
in Lacedaemon and in Thebes; and in the games
they put their hands to the greatest number of contests,
and graced their houses with tripods, cauldrons, and
    golden bowls,
whenever they tasted the crowns of victory.
Their excellence shines out with brightness
in both naked races and in the contests where armed men run,
their shields clattering; and also when they threw javelins
from their hands, and when they flung discuses of stone—
for the pentathlon did not exist, but a prize was given for each event.

Often they bound their hair with close-knit garlands from
    these games,
and appeared in glory beside Dirce's waters and by the Eurotas:*
one of them Iphicles' son,* of the same race as the Sown Men,*   30
the other Tyndareus' son,* who lived among the Achaeans
in his house on the high plateau of Therapne.

Farewell to you; but as I wrap my robe of song about Poseidon
and the sacred Isthmus, and Onchestus' shores,*
I shall as I honour this man speak of the glorious fate of his father
Asopodorus, and his ancestral lands in Orchomenus,
which have welcomed him back from a boundless sea,
when he was oppressed by shipwreck and chill calamity.
But now his family's Destiny has again established him
in the fair weather of former times.   40

The man who has toiled with understanding also wins foresight;
and if he dedicates his whole heart to excellence,
employing both expense and effort,
we must with an ungrudging spirit
grant him a proud boast if he achieves it.
For it is a trifling offering if a skilled poet,
speaking a good word to mark many great labours,
erects a splendid memorial in which all may share.

Different rewards bring pleasure to men for different deeds:
the shepherd, the ploughman, the bird-trapper,
the man whose livelihood is in the sea;
for all men strain to keep persistent hunger from their bellies.
But the greatest profit is earned by the man
who wins splendid glory in war or in the games,   50
through praise, which is the choicest address
from the tongues of citizens and strangers.

As for us, we must sing of our neighbour, Cronus' son the
    Earthshaker,*
lord of the running horses, to repay his aid in the chariot race;
and we must call upon your sons, Amphitryon,* and the vale
    of Minyas,*
and Demeter's famous grove at Eleusis,* and Euboea's twisting
    racecourse.*

To these, Protesilaus,* I add your precinct at Phylace of the
  men of Achaea.

But to give a full account of the successes   60
which Hermes, god of the games, has granted Herodotus
is precluded by the brief measure of my song.
In truth, what is passed over in silence often brings greater
  happiness.
May he, lifted up on the tuneful Pierians'* bright wings,
still yet wreathe his hand with prized garlands
from Pytho and from the Alpheus at Olympia,
bringing honour to seven-gated Thebes.
If a man keeps his wealth hidden indoors,
laughing scornfully at others, he does not realize
that he will render up his soul to Hades unattended by fame.

ISTHMIAN 2

For Xenocrates of Acragas, winner of the chariot race

When, Thrasybulus, poets of former times* took the
    splendid lyre
and mounted the chariot of the golden-circleted Muses,
they would lightly shoot their honey-voiced love songs at
    any boy
whose alluring late-summer beauty could woo fair-throned
    Aphrodite.
For the Muse was not yet greedy for gain, nor worked for hire,
nor did sweet soft-voiced songs with silvered faces
offer themselves for sale, peddled by honey-voiced Terpsichore.*
But today she orders us to bear in mind the Argive's saying,*
which comes very close to the truth: 10
'Money it is, money that makes the man,'
said the man deserted by both possessions and friends.

No more of that, for you are wise, and not unknown to you
is the Isthmian chariot victory of which I sing,
which Poseidon awarded Xenocrates,
and sent him a crown of Dorian wild celery to wreathe in his hair,
honouring an expert charioteer, a splendour for the men
    of Acragas.
Mighty Apollo saw him at Crisa,* and also gave him glory there;
and in shining Athens, revelling in the famed favour of the
    Erechtheidae,*   20
he found no fault with the chariot-protecting hand with which
    Nicomachus,*
whipper of horses, precisely handled all his reins;
whom also the heralds of the seasons announced—
the Eleans, truce-holders* of Zeus the son of Cronus,
who doubtless had enjoyed some act of guest-friendship.
They welcomed him with sweet-breathing voices when he fell
on golden Victory's knees in their country
which men call the grove of Olympian Zeus,
where the sons of Aenesidamus* enjoyed immortal honours;

for indeed your house, Thrasybulus, is not unacquainted 30
with pleasing victory revels or with honeyed songs of pride.

For no hill lies in the way, nor is the road steep
when one brings the honours of the Heliconian goddesses*
to the houses of distinguished men.
I have thrown the discus far; may I now cast my javelin
as far as Xenocrates outstripped other men
in the sweetness of his disposition.
Respected in the company of his fellow townsmen,
he observed the Panhellenic code in his horse-rearing practice,
and welcomed every feast of the gods* with open arms.
No wind's contrary blast forced him to furl the sails 40
at his hospitable table; in summer he would go as far as Phasis,*
and in winter to the shore of the Nile.

Envious expectations hang around mortals' minds.
Do not then allow this man to be silent about his father's virtues,
nor about these hymns—for certainly I did not shape them to
    stand still.
Make these words known to him, Nicasippus,*
when you encounter my estimable guest-friend.

ISTHMIAN 3

For Melissus of Thebes, winner of the chariot race

If a man is successful
either in far-famed games or in the power of wealth,
and stifles restless excess in his heart,
he deserves to enjoy his fellow townsmen's praise.
Zeus, from you come great accomplishments to mortals;
their happiness lives longer when they are righteous,
but does not equally prosper for all time
when it keeps company with crooked minds.
To reward a good man's illustrious deeds
we must both sing hymns for him and, as he revels in victory,
raise him up with the gentle charm of poetry.

Melissus' good fortune has brought him a second prize
which may incline his heart toward pleasurable rejoicing;   10
he won one crown in the dales of Isthmus, and then
in the low-lying valley of the deep-chested lion*
he caused Thebe to be proclaimed by his chariot victory.
He does not disgrace the inborn excellence of his family.
You here must surely know the ancient fame
of Cleonymus* and his chariots; and on their mother's side
these men shared in the wealth of Labdacus' clan*
and trod the strenuous path of four-horsed chariot racing.

Life, as the days roll past, changes now in this way and now
   in that,
and only the sons of the gods steer clear of wounds.

ISTHMIAN 4

For Melissus of Thebes, winner in the pancration

By the gods' favour, Melissus, there are myriad paths leading
    everywhere,
which I can follow to hymn your family's successes,
since you have revealed a full store of them to me at the Isthmus.
Through these the Cleonymids* continually flourish, with
    a god's help,
as they live their mortal lives through to their end.
Different winds blow hard on all mankind
at different times, driving them on.
But these men have been honoured in Thebes since its
    beginning,
it is said, as friendly hosts to its surrounding peoples,
for they lack strident arrogance; and as for the testimonials
of boundless fame that are blown by winds among men, living
    and dead,   10
these they have attained in entirety, and by their outstanding
    manly deeds
have from their home touched the pillars of Heracles.*
Do not any longer strive for farther-flung success.

They were horse-rearers, and gained the approval of brazen Ares;
but for all that, on one day a cruel snowstorm of war*
robbed their hallowed hearth of four men.
Yet now in its turn, after the darkness of winter's months,
it is as if the variegated earth has by the gods' design
flowered with red roses. He who makes the earth tremble,
whose seat is Onchestus* and the sea-bridge before
    Corinth's walls,   20
by awarding this wonderful hymn to the family
rouses the ancient glory of famous deeds from its bed.
It had fallen asleep, but is now awakened,
and its skin shines out like the Morning Star,*
brilliant to look upon among the other stars.
This ancient fame proclaimed their chariot's victory

both on Athens' slopes and in Adrastus' games at Sicyon,*
and awarded them leaves of song such as these from poets
     of that time.
Nor did they withhold their curved chariot from national festivals,
but gladly laid out expenditure on horses, in competition with
     all the Hellenes.
Those who take no part endure the silence of anonymity;   30
but even those who do compete are invisible to fortune
until they attain the final goal,
for she hands out to men a share of both good and bad,
and lesser men's cunning can overtake their betters and make
     them stumble.

You must know of the courage of Ajax,*
which in the dead of night he cut through and bloodied with
     his sword,
and brought reproach to the sons of the Hellenes who went
     to Troy.
But Homer, we know, has honoured him among men,
in that he has set straight his whole achievement
and made it known with his staff* of wonderful verses
for later men to use as themes in song.
For if a man says something well   40
it spreads abroad as an immortal utterance,
and the ever-unquenched brilliance of noble deeds
ranges over the fruitful earth and the sea.

May we find the Muses in sympathetic mood,
and so kindle such a beacon of hymns also for Melissus,
scion of Telesiadas—a crown worthy of a pancratiast—
for in the fight his courage resembles the daring of loud-roaring
mountain lions, and in cunning he is like the fox,
which spreads itself backwards to block the eagle's onrush.
One must use every stratagem to weaken one's opponent's strength;
for he was not granted the physique of an Orion,*
yet though he is of puny appearance   50
his strength makes him a hard man to overcome.

Indeed, a man short in stature but of unyielding spirit
once went from Cadmean Thebes to the house of Antaeus*

in wheat-bearing Libya, to wrestle with him
and stop him roofing Poseidon's temple with strangers' skulls.
This was Alcmene's son, who after he had ranged over
the surface of the entire earth and the grey sea's
    steep-cliffed bowl,
and cleared its passage for sailors, went to Olympus,
where now he lives next to the Aegis-bearer,*
enjoying supreme happiness, and is honoured as the gods'
    friend;
married to Hebe, he is lord of a golden palace and son-in-law
    to Hera.   60

For him we citizens prepare a feast beyond the Electran Gates,*
and a newly built circle of altars, heaping up burnt offerings
in honour of the bronze-armoured eight who died,
the sons borne to him by Megara, daughter of Creon.

For them at sunset a flame leaps up and burns all night,
kicking the heavens with its savoury smoke.
On the second day is the conclusion of the yearly games,
the work of strength. Here this man, his hair whitened
    with myrtle,
displayed a double victory, and a third before this as a boy,   70
obedient to the copious advice of his oar-guiding helmsman.
I shall join Orseas* with him in my revel song,
showering them with this hymn's delight.

ISTHMIAN 5

For Phylacidas of Aegina, winner in the pancration

Many-titled Theia, mother of the Sun;* because of you
all men reckon gold to be powerful beyond other things.
So also it is through the honour you give them, O queen,
that ships which battle on the sea
or horses harnessed to chariots
arouse admiration in swiftly wheeling contests.

And in athletic competitions too a man wins longed-for glory
when many crowns have bound his hair
for victories gained by hands or swiftness of feet.   10
But men's prowess is decided by the gods;
truly, two things only shepherd life to its sweetest perfection:
if a man is blessed with flourishing prosperity,
and if he enjoys a noble reputation.
Do not seek to become Zeus;
if a share of these blessings comes to you, you possess everything.
Mortal ways suit mortal men.

For you, Phylacidas, the flower of double success is recorded
at the Isthmus and at Nemea, both for you
and for Pytheas, in the pancration.
But my heart can taste no hymns if I omit the Aeacids.   20
I have come with the Graces to this well-ordered city
for the sake of Lampon's sons; once a man sets his foot
on the clear path of god-given achievements,
do not hold back from blending apt boasts into your song,
in recognition of former labours.
For among heroes too noble fighters have merited praise,
and they have been celebrated for countless ages on the lyre
and on the many-voiced music of pipes. By Zeus' ordinance
reverence for them has given skilled poets their theme:
in the Aetolians' bright sacrifices Oeneus' mighty sons* are
    honoured,
and at Thebes Iolaus the charioteer; Perseus at Argos,   30
and the spear-fighters Castor and Polydeuces by Eurotas' streams.

But in Oenone* it is the great-hearted spirit of Aeacus and
    his sons,
who twice in battle sacked the city of Troy,*
first in Heracles' expedition and later with the sons of Atreus.

Now, lift my gaze up from the plain!*
Tell me, who were Cycnus' killers, and who Hector's?
Memnon's* too, the Ethiopians' fearless bronze-armoured
    chieftain?   40
Who wounded noble Telephus* with his spear by
    Caicus' banks?
My mouth proclaims Aegina, famous island, as their
    fatherland;
from ancient times it has stood, built as a tower
for men to scale by means of lofty exploits.
My tongue, ready with words, has many arrows
to sound out in their praise; and in the recent war
Ajax' city Salamis could testify to being saved by its sailors
in Zeus' lethal rainstorm, a fall of bloody hail on
    numberless men.   50

But stop, drench that boast in silence!
It is Zeus who deals out good and bad, Zeus the master of all.
Honours such as these* also delight in victory's joy,
accompanied by the honeyed pleasure of song.
Let him who struggles to perform in the games
learn well about the family of Cleonicus;*
their men's long toil is not lost in obscurity,
nor has great expenditure worn down their fervent hopes.
I praise Pytheas too among body-tamers
for setting Phylacidas' blows on a straight course—   60
skilful with his hands, and a match for him in judgement.
Take up a crown for him, bring him a headband of fine wool,
and with them send forth this new winged hymn.

ISTHMIAN 6

For Phylacidas of Aegina, winner in the boys' pancration

As men do at the height of a symposium,*
so we mix a second bowl of the Muses' songs
for Lampon's family of outstanding athletes.
They first won the finest of crowns at Nemea,
Zeus, through your favour, and now again
with the aid of the Isthmus' master and the fifty Nereids
Phylacidas, his youngest son, has been victorious.
May we have a third libation to offer the Olympian saviour,
to be poured with honey-voiced songs over Aegina!
For if a man takes delight in toil and expenditure,   10
and so succeeds in god-framed exploits,
and if a divine power plants in him the pleasure of fame,
he drops his anchor at the furthest limits of happiness,
honoured by the gods. With feelings such as these
    Cleonicus' son*
prays to encounter Hades and to accept grey old age;
I appeal to Clotho* on her high throne, and her sister Fates,
to agree with the noble commands of my friend.

As for you, golden-charioted descendants of Aeacus,
I proclaim that my clearest charge as I come to your island   20
is to rain down praises upon it.
Numberless paths, one hundred feet wide,
have been laid out by your illustrious deeds, one after the other,
beyond the source of the Nile and further than the
    Hyperboreans;*
and there is no city so barbarous or of such crude speech
that it has not heard of the fame of the hero Peleus,*
blessed son-in-law of the gods; or of Ajax Telamon's son,
or of his father, who, an eager ally, was taken in ships
with the men of Tiryns to bronze-loving war at Troy—
a heroes' struggle—by Alcmene's son,* because of
    Laomedon's crimes.
He stormed Pergamus, and with Telamon   30

slew the people of the Meropes and the oxherd Alcyoneus,*
huge as a mountain, when he met him at Phlegrae,*
nor did he—Heracles—keep his hands from his deep-voiced
   bowstring.

But when he came to summon Aeacus' son* to the expedition
he found them feasting. As Amphitryon's son,
the mighty spearman, stood there in his lion's pelt,
incomparable Telamon held out to him a wine cup
encrusted with gold, and invited him to pour the first nectar
   libation.   40
Heracles raised his unconquerable hands to the heaven
   and spoke:
'Father Zeus, if ever you heard my prayers with a willing heart,
now, now, I entreat you to bring to birth from Eriboea
a daring son for this man, to be my destined guest-friend.
Make his body as indestructible as this hide which now
   enfolds me,
taken from the beast which long ago I killed in Nemea
as the very first of my labours; and may his courage be equal to it!'

He spoke; and the god sent a great eagle, the lord of birds,   50
and the thrill of sweet joy entered him.
Then like a prophet he declared:
'Telamon, you shall have the son you ask for.
Following the portent of this bird, call him Ajax* the powerful,
awesome among men in the struggles of Enyalius.'*

So he spoke, and quickly sat down. To rehearse all their exploits
would be too long a task, since I have come, Muse,
to marshal the revels for Phylacidas, and for Pytheas and
   Euthymenes;*
and so, in the Argive manner,* my tale will be very brief.
At the Isthmus they won three victories in the pancration,   60
and others at leafy Nemea, these brilliant boys and their uncle.
What hymns have they brought to light, to be their allotted
   portion!
They refresh the Psalychiad line with the Graces' finest dew,
and inhabiting this god-loved city they have exalted the house
   of Themistius.*

Lampon, showing zeal in his task, truly honours Hesiod's
   maxim,*
and quotes it with approval to his sons;
he embellishes his city for the benefit of all,
and is esteemed for his hospitality to strangers;   70
he strives for due measure in judgement, and holds fast to it.
Nor does his tongue leave his thoughts behind;
you would say that this man in the company of athletes
is a Naxian whetstone* among other stones, a tamer of bronze.
To them I shall give to drink the holy water of Dirce,*
which the deep-girdled daughters of Mnemosyne
have caused to gush out near Cadmus' well-walled gates.

ISTHMIAN 7

For Strepsiades of Thebes, winner in the pancration

In which of your land's past glories, blessed Thebe,*
does your heart take especial pleasure?
Was it your exaltation of Dionysus, with his
    loose-flowing hair,
to be an associate of Demeter* of the clanging bronze?
Or was it when you received the mightiest of the gods
at midnight in a snowstorm of gold,*
at the time when he stood in the doorway of Amphitryon,
in pursuit of his wife for the birth of Heracles?
Or was it because of Teiresias* and his subtle counsels?
Or was it because of Iolaus,* skilled handler of horses?
Or was it the Sown Men,* with their unfaltering spears?   10
Or was it when you drove Adrastus,* stripped of his myriad
    companions,
back from the violent shouts of battle to Argos land of horses?
Or when you founded the Dorian colony of Lacedaemon
on a firm footing, and when your descendants the Aegeidae
took Amyclae in obedience to the Pythian oracles?*

But no more of that. The ancient brilliance sleeps,
and mortals are unaware of all that does not reach
poetry's finest flower, yoked to splendid streams of verse.

Therefore make revel for Strepsiades too with
    sweet-voiced hymns,   20
for he is victorious in the pancration at the Isthmus;
of amazing strength and handsome to look upon,
he wins a distinction which does not shame his beauty.
He is bathed in the brightness of the violet-haired Muses,
and he has given a share in his crown to his namesake uncle,
whom Ares of the bronze shield conveyed to his doom.
But for brave men honour is stored up as their reward.
Let all know clearly, who in a cloud of battle such as this
defend their beloved land from the hail of blood,
keeping destruction at bay in the face of the enemy,

that they raise their fellow townsmen's fame to the highest
   degree,
both in their lives and after they are dead.   30

Just so you, son of Diodotus,* followed the example
of the warrior Meleager, and of Hector and Amphiaraus,*
breathing out the full bloom of your life
as you fought in the forefront of the tumult,
where the bravest bore the brunt of battle's strife
at the limit of their hopes. The grief I suffered
was too great for words, but now the Earth-holder*
has granted me calm after the storm, and I shall sing,
binding garlands in my hair. May the immortals' envy
not bring about disorder because I pursue the pleasure of
   the day   40
and walk quietly towards old age and my fated span of life.

For we all alike die, but our destinies are not the same.
If a man gazes on faraway things he is nevertheless
too weak to reach the bronze-floored house of the gods.
Indeed, when Bellerophon desired to enter heaven's stables
to join the company of Zeus, winged Pegasus* threw his
   master off;
a most bitter end awaits the sweetness of unlawful joys.
Even so, Loxias* exulting in your luxuriant golden hair, may
   you yet bestow
on us a fine-flowering crown in your games at Pytho.   50

ISTHMIAN 8

For Cleandrus of Aegina, winner in the pancration

On behalf of Cleandrus and his youthful prime, O young men,
let someone go to the bright portal of his father Telesarchus
and wake the revel that is glorious recompense for his toil:
both for his victory at the Isthmus
and because at Nemea he gained ascendancy in the contest.

So I too, though my heart grieves, am invited to invoke
    the golden Muse.
We have been delivered from great distress,
but we must not let ourselves be denied crowns;
nor should you nurse your anxieties.
No, now that we are relieved of our intractable troubles
let us also after labours sing a sweet civic song,
since Tantalus' stone*—an intolerable labour for Hellas—   10
has been shifted by some god from above our heads.
But fear arising from past events holds back my strong
    ambition;
it is best to keep one's eyes always on each thing before
    one's feet,
for over men hangs a deceptive existence, as it unwinds
    life's path.
Yet even for this mortals may find a cure, if only they have
    freedom;
men must keep good hope in mind, and one raised in
    seven-gated Thebes
should hold out the flower of the Graces to Aegina,
for these twins were the youngest daughters of Asopus,*
and they found favour with Zeus the king.

One he settled by Dirce's beautiful waters as ruler of
    a chariot-loving city,   20
while you he conducted to Oenopia's island* and lay with you,
and there you gave birth to glorious Aeacus,*
dearest of mortals to his deep-thundering father,
who settled disputes even for the immortals.

His godlike sons and their sons, lovers of battle,
were counted the bravest in the exercise of the groaning tumult
of brazen war. Yet they were temperate, and prudent in heart.
This also the assembled gods remembered, when Zeus
and glorious Poseidon wrangled over marriage to Thetis,
each wishing her to be his beautiful wife,
for desire had taken hold of them.
But the gods' immortal wits did not deliver her to their bed,   30
since they were obedient to the decree of fate;
for wise Themis said in their assembly that it was ordained
that the sea-goddess would bear a princely son,
mightier than his father,* whose hand would hurl
a weapon greater than thunderbolt or invincible trident,
if she was to couple with Zeus or with his brothers.

'Come, you must put an end to this! Let her enjoy a
    mortal's bed,
and see her son die in battle, equal to Ares in his hands'
    strength,
and to the lightning in the swiftness of his feet.
This is my advice: give her in marriage as a god-sent prize
to Peleus son of Aeacus, who they say is
the most god-fearing man to be raised on Iolcus' plain.   40
Let this message go at once straight to Chiron's*
    everlasting cave,
that Nereus' daughter must not once again place in our hands
the voting-leaves of dissension, but on some evening of the
    full moon
let her, in submission to that hero, untie her virginity's
    lovely bridle.'

So spoke the goddess in counsel to the children of Cronus,
and they nodded approval with their immortal brows.
Nor did the fruit of her words wither away; they say that
    the king*
agreed with the rest to this marriage for Thetis,
and poets' mouths have revealed to the ignorant
Achilles' youthful exploits: how he bloodied Mysia's
    vine-clad plain,
drenching it in Telephus'* dark gore; how he built a bridge   50

for the Atreids' return and rescued Helen; how with his spear
he sliced through the sinews of Troy, which before this
had prevented him from ordering the work of manslaying battle
on the plain: violent Memnon, proud Hector, and other chieftains.
These Achilles showed the way to the house of Persephone—
he the bulwark of the Aeacids—glorifying Aegina and his roots.
Not even in death did songs desert him; the maidens
    of Helicon*
stood by his pyre and tomb and poured over him a
    many-voiced dirge,
and the gods too resolved that noble men should become
a theme for the hymns of these goddesses, even after
    their death.   60

And that rule still holds good today, as the chariot of the Muses
makes haste to sing a loud song for Nicocles,* to remember
    his boxing.
Honour him all of you: the man who in the valley of the Isthmus
was awarded the crown of Dorian wild celery; for in time
    gone by
he too overcame men who lived round about, beating them down
with fists which none could escape.
Nor is he shamed by the line of his father's excellent brother;
therefore let one of his companions plait a welcome crown
    of myrtle
for Cleandrus in recognition of his pancration,
since in time past Alcathous'* games and Epidaurus' young men
welcomed him with good fortune.
The good man has reason to praise him, for he has not
    suppressed his youth   70
in obscurity,* being unacquainted with fine deeds.

EXPLANATORY NOTES

OLYMPIAN 1

O. 1 celebrates the victory of Hieron, tyrant of Syracuse, in the single-horse race of 476 BC. He won three times at the Olympic games and three times at the Pythian games between 482 and 468. Pindar celebrates one of his Pythian victories in *P.* 1. Like *P.* 2, composed in the same year, this poem begins with a magnificent 'priamel' or build-up to a resounding climax. The myth of Tantalus at the centre may be intended as a veiled reminder to Hieron not to overstep the mark.

1 *Water is best*: perhaps because it shines most or because it is essential in a hot country.

7 *Olympia*: venue for the Olympic games.

9 *poets*: Aeschylus, Simonides, and Bacchylides also composed for Hieron.

10 *son of Cronus*: Zeus, in whose honour the Olympic games were held, and from whom rulers derived their authority.

17 *Dorian*: the Dorians were the early inhabitants of Western Greece; at *P.* 1.62–6 Pindar says Hieron founded Aetna with a Dorian constitution. The point here is probably that his ode is tailored to suit Hieron; cf. *O.* 3.5 and *P.* 1.61–5.

18 *Pisa*: the district in which Olympia was situated.

18 *Pherenicus*: 'Victory-winner', Hieron's victorious horse.

20 *Alpheus*: river flowing through Olympia.

24 *the land / of fine men*: the Peloponnese ('island of Pelops').

24 *Lydian Pelops*: Pelops came from Lydia, a territory in Asia Minor bordering the Aegean Sea, but he had a famous tomb at Olympia (lines 93–4 below) and his chariot race to win Hippodameia (below, 70) featured on the Temple of Zeus there. His strong connections with Olympia make him an appropriate subject of the myth in *O.* 1.

26 *Clotho*: one of the three Fates. Pindar here alludes to the story he tells in more detail below (lines 36–51), how Pelops was served up to the gods by his wicked father Tantalus. Demeter ate one of his shoulders but it was replaced with an ivory one, and Poseidon fell in love with him.

26 *purifying cauldron*: alluding to Pindar's rejection (line 52 below) of the traditional story about Pelops.

38 *Sipylus*: in Lydia, where Tantalus lived.

40 *God of the Glorious Trident*: Poseidon.

44 *Ganymede*: carried off by Zeus to become his cup-bearer.

54 *watchers on Olympus*: the Olympian gods.

55 *Tantalus*: one of three sinners, along with Ixion and Sisyphus, who had eternal punishment in the Underworld. Pindar alludes again to his punishment by an overhanging stone at *I*. 8.10. Homer's version of his punishment (*Odyssey* 11.582–92), that he was forever trying to get food and drink that eluded him, is the familiar one.

70 *Hippodameia*: 'Horse-tamer'.

72–3 *deep-roaring Lord of the Trident*: Poseidon.

75 *Cypris*: Aphrodite.

78 *Elis*: location of Olympia.

90–1 *splendid blood-offerings*: Pelops was worshipped as a hero at Olympia: a black ram was sacrificed to him, and its blood allowed to trickle through the earth; Pelops would imbibe the blood and be vitalized and thus continue to assert his power.

102 *Aeolian melody*: the Aeolians were early inhabitants of parts of northern Greece, including Pindar's home-district of Boeotia (Thucydides 7.57.5). The reference here is obscure, but may either be to a particular musical mode or harmony or, more simply, mean 'in my musical style' (Aeoladas is the name of a man from Pindar's home-town Thebes in Pindar, *Parth*. 1.12, 2.9; for translations of *Partheneia* or *Maiden Songs*, see the Loeb edition of Pindar, ed. W. H. Race, ii. 320–31).

111 *hill of Cronus*: overlooking Olympia.

OLYMPIAN 2

O. 2, like *O*. 3, is for Theron, tyrant of Acragas in Sicily, who won the four-horse chariot race at Olympia in 476; he did not drive the chariot himself, but employed a charioteer, Nicomachus, mentioned at *I*. 2.22–4. He was a rival to Hieron for power in Sicily, and relationships between the two were volatile, though his niece became Hieron's third wife. Much of the ode is about death and the afterlife, themes of special relevance to an inhabitant of Acragas because it was a centre for Pythagoreans, who believed in metempsychosis. The poet-philosopher Empedocles, Theron's contemporary and also from Acragas, was a follower of the sect; some of his poetry, and some sections of the Orphic/Pythagorean gold leaves, found predominantly in southern Italy and giving ritual instructions to the dead relating to the afterlife, share Pindar's mystical eschatology.

2 *which god, which hero—which man*: echoed by Ezra Pound in his wistful poem 'E. P. Ode Pour L'Election de Son Sepulchre': O bright Apollo, | *Tin andra, tin heroa, tina theon*, | What god, man, or hero | Shall I place a tin wreath upon!'

8 *laboured hard*: alluding to the efforts involved in founding Acragas by Theron's ancestors who came from Rhodes (cf. Pindar, Frag. 119, Thucydides 6.4.3).

12 *Son of Cronus and Rhea*: Zeus.

16 *right or wrong*: perhaps alluding to a family feud between Theron and Hieron centred round Theron's daughter.

23 *daughters of Cadmus*: Semele, mother of Dionysus, who died when Zeus came to her as a flash of lightning, and Ino, who jumped into the sea to escape her mad husband and became a Nereid. The fate of Ino foreshadows the reflections on the afterlife that follow. Their father, Cadmus, was king of Thebes, and, according to an ancient commentator (Sch. *O.* 2.39), Pindar in another poem for Theron said that Cadmus was Theron's ancestor (Frag. 118).

29 *Nereus*: sea-god, father of the Nereids.

38 *Laius' son*: Oedipus, descendant of Cadmus; his sons, Eteocles and Polynices, died fighting each other, as told in Aeschylus' *Seven against Thebes*; Thersandrus, son of Polynices and the daughter of Adrastus, survived to save the family line.

46 *the son of Aenesidamus*: Theron.

49 *brother*: Xenocrates, who won the chariot race at the Pythian and Isthmian games (see *P.* 6 and *I.* 2).

56 *If a man possesses wealth, and knows the future*—: the 'if'clause is left unanswered. In what follows about the afterlife (down to line 86, 'they require interpreters'), many of the eschatological details are unclear to us, but Pindar suggests that to members of the Pythagorean cult the meaning will be clear enough. Some of the details are similar to those in the eschatological Orphic/Pythagorean gold leaves from southern Italy and elsewhere, which also seem to be deliberately obscure in order that the truth should remain known only to those belonging to the sect.

61–2 *the nights and sunny days / are in perpetual equal balance*: a permanent equinox.

71–2 *island of the blessed*: where heroes of special status dwell.

75 *Rhadamanthys*: judge in the Underworld appointed by Cronus, husband of Rhea.

82 *Cycnus*: son of Poseidon.

83 *the Ethiopian, son of the dawn*: Memnon.

88 *the divine bird of Zeus*: the eagle.

OLYMPIAN 3

This ode was probably performed at a *theoxenia*, a cult banquet for gods, honouring Castor, his twin-brother Polydeuces, and their sister Helen, children of Tyndareus, in thanks for Theron's chariot-race victory of 476 (cf. line 40; for another *theoxenia* see note to *N.* 10.39–40). There were several occasions when Pindar composed both a longer and a shorter ode for the same victory: besides *O.* 2 and *O.* 3 there are *P.* 4 and *P.* 5, *O.* 10 and *O.* 11, and perhaps *I.* 3 and *I.* 4. *O.* 3 lacks the sombre and predominantly moral tone of *O.* 2 and has a more regular mythical section. As is generally the case with Pindar's odes, one can only speculate about the circumstances surrounding *O. 3*'s composition, but perhaps after receiving *O. 2* Theron requested from Pindar a more fitting celebration of his victory (cf. lines 6–9).

3 *never-wearying hoofs*: the chariot race at Olympia was probably about 9 miles long!

5 *Dorian measure*: see note on *O. 1.17*.

9 *Aenesidamus' son*: Theron.

12 *Hellene judge ... of Aetolian stock*: one of the Elean judges (Hellanodicae) at the Olympic games; 'Aetolian' because the Eleans are here regarded as originating from Aetolia, the district of Greece north of the Corinthian Gulf.

14 *Amphitryon's son*: Heracles.

14 *Istrus'*: the river Danube.

16 *Hyperborean people*: a fabulous people of the far north, among whom Apollo spent the winter (cf. *P. 10.29–46*).

19 *father*: Zeus, in whose honour the Olympic games were held.

26 *Leto's daughter*: Artemis.

29 *Eurystheus'*: king of Argos who imposed on Heracles his twelve labours, one of which was to catch the golden hind which Taygeta had consecrated to Artemis (Orthosia) in thanks for the goddess having protected her from Zeus' amorous advances.

38 *Emmenidae*: Theron's family.

42 *If water is best*: cf. *O. 1.1–2*, an unusual self-reference by Pindar. *O. 1* and *O. 3* were composed at about the same time for two mutually acquainted tyrants, and Pindar is here tactfully implying that Theron is as great as Hieron. What follows suggests a parallel between Heracles and Theron: in winning at Olympia Theron has achieved the limit of human achievement, as Heracles did in journeying to the distant Hyperboreans, but he must remember that he is a mortal and cannot go too far; even Heracles had to come back.

OLYMPIAN 4

O. 4 (probably for a victory in the chariot race in 452) and *O. 5* are for Psaumis of Camarina in south Sicily. Lines 9–12 suggest that *O. 4* was designed as a prelude to a celebratory revel in which Psaumis rode crowned with his victory wreath through the city.

1 *Zeus*: Pindar represents him both as a chariot driver and as father of the seasons (cf. Hesiod, *Theogony* 901), including the one in which the Olympics were held (late summer).

7 *Typhos'*: a giant, subdued by Zeus, believed to be imprisoned beneath Aetna and to be responsible for its volcanic eruptions (cf. *P. 1.15–28*).

11 *It comes*: the procession.

16 *Concord*: Hesychia, personification of political peace. Pindar alludes to Camarina's constant disputes with Syracuse; it was destroyed by the Syracusans in 533, again in the 480s, and re-established in 461 about a decade before this ode.

19 *son of Clymenus*: Erginus, one of the Argonauts, who won the race in armour at games put on by the women of Lemnos when the Argonauts stopped there. An ancient commentator (Sch. *O.* 4.29b; cf. 39a, b) wrote, 'it is clear that Psaumis himself too won when he was already grey-haired'; if so, there would be more point to the episode as told by Pindar.

OLYMPIAN 5

This ode is probably not by Pindar: an ancient commentator (*O.* 5 Inscr.a) reports that it was not transmitted along with the rest of the odes but attributed to Pindar in the commentaries of the first century BC Alexandrian scholar Didymus. The language varies between odd and naive. It seems to celebrate a victory in the mule race (cf. line 3), which was part of the Olympic programme from 500 to 444 and was specially promoted by the mule-breeding Sicilians; but its date is uncertain, though probably shortly after the rebuilding of Camarina in 461 (cf. line 8). The ode suggests that Psaumis was also a wealthy horse-breeder and had helped in the restoration of the city.

2 *daughter of Oceanus*: alluding to the nearby lake, also called Camarina (cf. line 11).

3 *tireless-footed*: imitated from *O.* 4.1.

5 *six double-altars*: cf. *O.* 10.25 where Heracles is said to have established them. There were numerous altars at Olympia (cf. Pausanias 5.14–15).

10 *Pallas*: Athene, who had a temple overlooking the city.

9–10 *dwellings of Pelops and Oenomaus*: Olympia.

12 *Hipparis*: Camarina was at the mouth of the river by the sea.

13 *constructs a lofty grove of well-built houses*: a most oddly expressed description.

18 *Ida's holy cave*: probably a reference to Mt. Ida on Crete where Zeus was brought up and worshipped.

19 *Lydian pipes*: Plato describes certain Lydian modes as relaxed and suitable for drinking-songs (*Republic* 398e).

OLYMPIAN 6

Like *O.* 5, composed for a victory in the mule-cart race. The victor, Hagesias, came from Stymphalis in Arcadia, central Peloponnese, but lived, like Hieron, in Syracuse. The victory was in 476, 472, or 468, Olympic games when Hieron was in power (cf. line 93). Hagesias was an official (line 5) in charge of the oracle of Zeus at Olympia, consulted by athletes before they took part in the games (*O.* 8.1–7), a hereditary post held by members of the prophetic clan of the Iamidae, to which Hagesias must have belonged. The main myth in the poem explains how the clan's ancestor, Iamus, acquired his prophetic gifts.

5 *prophetic altar of Zeus*: see note on *O*. 8.3.

6 *joint founder*: Hagesias was not a founder of Syracuse, so the Greek should perhaps be interpreted to mean 'co-inhabitant' (i.e. of Syracuse and Stymphalis).

9 *Sostratus' son*: Hagesias.

13 *Adrastus . . . Amphiaraus*: Adrastus (son of Talaus) and Amphiaraus were two of the Seven against Thebes. As a seer, Amphiaraus is a suitable parallel to Hagesias; having been swallowed up by the earth, he was consulted as an oracle under the ground. A scholiast (*O*. 6.30c) suggests not implausibly that Hagesias took part in military campaigns with Hieron and helped him as both seer and soldier.

22 *Phintis*: probably the driver of the mule-cart.

28 *Pitane*: the name of both a district (of Sparta) and the associated heroine. The myth that follows, explaining the origins of the victor's prophetic clan, the Iamids, has been deliberately tailored by Pindar to straddle both Olympia and Sparta, because at the time *O*. 6 was composed the most famous Iamid was Tisamenus of Elis who became a Spartan citizen (Herodotus 9.33–6).

28 *Eurotas*: river at Sparta.

33 *Aepytus, the hero son of Eilatus*: Pindar says that Aepytus rules the Arcadians, even though Phaesane, where he ruled, seems to have been in Elis (not part of Arcadia). However, the river Alpheus, where (vaguely) he lived, flowed through both Arcadia and Elis (and Olympia). The overall effect of this geographical fudging is to make Aepytus, like Hagesias, have connections with both Arcadia and Olympia.

41 *the golden-haired god*: Apollo, who, by ensuring that a gentle birth-goddess (Eleithyia) and the Fates are present, indicates that a special child is to be born.

46–7 *blameless venom of bees*: honey.

57 *this immortal name*: Iamus, punning on the Greek for violets (*ia*).

64 *the steep rock of lofty Cronus' son*: hill of Cronus at Olympia.

66–7 *the voice that could not lie*: Pindar suggests that originally the Iamids prophesied by listening to the voice of Apollo (cf. *P*. 3.28–30).

68 *Alcidae*: Heracles' mortal father, Amphitryon, was son of Alceus.

70 *at the very top of Zeus' altar*: see note to *O*. 8.3.

77 *mountain of Cyllene*: in Arcadia, birthplace of Hermes, god of sport (cf. *P*. 2.10) and son of Zeus (the 'deep-thundering father', line 81).

84 *Metope*: daughter of Ladon, an Arcadian river (hence 'Stymphalian'), and wife of Asopus father of Thebe, eponymous heroine of Pindar's Thebes. Pindar here claims a connection between his own ancestry and the

victor's, as he seems to do also at *P.* 5.72–81. In his poems he links himself with the victors in many ways, by speaking in athletics metaphors, claiming divine inspiration, or warding off envious detractors, for example.

88 *Aeneas*: trainer of the chorus.

88 *Hera Parthenia*: Hera the Virgin. Hera was worshipped as the goddess of girls in a number of places, including Stymphalis. The mention is timely, if, as seems likely, *O.* 6 was (in the first instance) performed by a chorus of girls at Stymphalis, and has the effect of thanking the goddess for giving help to the chorus.

90 *'Boeotian pig'*: alluding to the Boeotians' proverbial rusticity.

91 *message-stick of the fair-haired Muses*: i.e. 'clever interpreter', far removed from Boeotian boorishness. To facilitate the conveyance of messages, the Spartans wrapped them round sticks, carrying them like a baton.

92 *Ortygia*: island off Syracuse.

95 *daughter*: Persephone.

96 *Zeus on Aetna*: Hieron refounded the Sicilian city of Catana, renaming it Aetna. Zeus watched over it carefully (cf. *P.* 1.30) as the monster Typhos, responsible for the volcano, was imprisoned underneath.

103 *Lord, master of the sea*: Poseidon. Pindar imagines the ode travelling to Hieron at Syracuse, where it was perhaps given a second performance.

OLYMPIAN 7

Rhodes produced some outstanding athletes: Leonidas who won all three running events at the Olympics on four successive occasions (164–152 BC), and Diagoras and his descendants who between them won seven Olympic titles in the boxing and pancration. Such was Diagoras' standing that *O.* 7, composed for him in 464, was engraved in gold letters and dedicated in the temple of Athene at Lindus, and there is a story that one of his daughters was uniquely allowed to be a female spectator at the Olympics (Drachmann's edition of the scholia on Pindar, i. 195–9). The ode is dominated by three myths concerning the founding of Rhodes.

9 *I propitiate them*: the Greek word is generally used only of appeasing the gods. The implication here is that Diagoras' victories set him above other men; a scholiast records a story of the Rhodians that he was a son of Hermes (Drachmann, i. 196, 199).

14 *Rhodes*: both island and eponymous nymph (cf. Pitane, *O.* 6.28).

17 *Castalia*: a spring at Delphi, so denoting the Pythian games.

18 *island of three cities*: Lindus, Ialysus, Camirus (cf. lines 73–4). This three-fold division, and what follows about Tlapolemus, is based essentially on *Iliad* 2.653–70.

23 *Zeus*: Tlapolemus' father was Heracles, son of Zeus; his mother was
    Astydameia, daughter of Amyntor. Licymnius was a great-uncle of
    Tlapolemus. The effect of this genealogizing is to highlight the nobility of
    the ancestors of Diagoras, a descendant of Tlapolemus.

27 *Alcmene's*: mother of Heracles.

29 *Midea's*: probably denoting Licymnius' mother, the concubine of Alcmene's
    father Electryon.

32 *golden-haired god*: Apollo.

33 *Lerna's*: near Argos.

33 *island pasture*: the island of Rhodes. What follows explains why there were
    fireless sacrifices at the temple of Athene at Lindus, and highlights the
    importance of the sun-god Helios (son of Hyperion) to whom the island
    was sacred (cf. lines 80–1). The Colossus of Rhodes, one of the Seven
    Wonders of the World, was a statue of the sun-god.

51 *the grey-eyed goddess*: Athene, who honoured the island by endowing it with
    skill and wisdom. The next sentences probably allude to the Telchines,
    mythical wizards who inhabited Rhodes and other islands and were espe-
    cially skilled in metalwork.

64 *Lachesis*: one of the three Fates.

79 *as if he were a god*: an exceptional honour, because he was the first colonizer
    of the island; similarly, Theagenes of Thasos, an exceptional boxer and
    pancratiast, was worshipped after his death as a god (Pausanias 6.11.8–9).
    Superhuman individuals could bridge the gulf between man and god.

80 *games*: the Tlepolemeia.

80 *Diagoras*: there follows a magnificent victory-list. He was a winner at each
    of the big four games — for the Pythian, see line 10, 'Delphi' — comparable
    to a winner nowadays in the Olympic, European, and Commonwealth
    Games, and World Championships.

83 *bronze*: the prize at Argos was probably a bronze shield, in Arcadia (at
    unspecified games) probably tripods.

87 *Atabyrion's*: Rhodes' highest mountain.

93 *Callianax*: ancestor of Diagoras, whose family clan was the Eratidae. As
    often, after praising a great victor Pindar adds a note of caution.

OLYMPIAN 8

Composed in 460 BC, this is one of eleven extant odes (more than a quarter of
the total that survive) that Pindar wrote for victors from the island of Aegina.
He admired their old-fashioned Dorian qualities (cf. line 30), their hospitality
(line 26), and there was kinship between Aegina and Pindar's home-city
of Thebes (*I.* 8.16–18: Aegina and Thebe are sister nymphs). Alcimedon,
the victor's name, means 'Strong-ruling'; the name of Timosthenes, probably

his brother, whose Nemean victory Pindar praises (lines 15–16), means 'Honouring strength', both good names for wrestlers.

3 *burnt offerings*: at Olympia the altar of Zeus consisted of the bonfire-heap created by the burning of sacrificial offerings; as the offerings were burnt, they were examined by the priest who pronounced an oracle according to his interpretation of what he saw. Athletes consulted the oracle to learn what their chances in the games were. For a graphic description of this sort of divination, pyromancy, cf. Sophocles, *Antigone* 1005–13. See also note to *O.* 6.5.

16 *Zeus as its protector*: as patron of both the Olympic and Nemean games where the brothers had won.

19 *Handsome . . . beauty*: Pindar regularly mentions the physical beauty of young victorious athletes; cf. *O.* 9.94, *N.* 3.19. They would be an attractive proposition to women (*P.* 9.97–100) and older men. Similarly, after Bob Mathias won the Olympic decathlon in 1948, 'The handsome young athlete received 200 offers of marriage' (*The Times*, 7 September 2006).

22 *Themis*: goddess of justice, exemplified by the Aeginetans in their hospitality.

31 *Leto's son*: Apollo. Aeacus, a local Aeginetan hero (son of Zeus and the eponymous nymph Aegina, *N.* 8.7), features strongly in Pindar's Aeginetan odes, often as ancestor to the famous exploits of the great Achilles, but his role here is a Pindaric invention (Sch. *O.* 8.41a) enabling Pindar to incorporate an oracle into the myth, thus thematically linking the myth to the opening of the ode.

42 *Pergamus*: Troy.

45–6 *in the first and fourth generations*: Troy was first captured by Aeacus' sons Peleus and Telamon, and again later by his great-grandson Neoptolemus, who by some suitably oracular maths is alluded to as (counting Aeacus himself) fourth-generation (Aeacus–Peleus/Telamon–Achilles/Ajax–Neoptolemus).

47 *Xanthus*: river in Lycia, Asia Minor (Amazon country), now south-west Turkey, not to be confused with the Trojan river Xanthus, the Scamander. The Ister is the Danube.

48 *trident-wielder*: a uniquely Pindaric term for Poseidon.

54 *Melesias'*: athletics coach of Alcimedon, who had himself won as a junior (beardless) and a man in the Nemean games. As nowadays, coaches tended to be ex-athletes.

69 *the bitterest of returns*: in the ancient games, there was generally no merit in anything other than victory, and nothing at the Olympics analogous to today's silver and bronze medals.

75 *Blepsiad clan*: the victor's family.

81–2 *Iphion . . . Callimachus*: deceased members of the victor's family, perhaps his father and uncle.

OLYMPIAN 9

Epharmostus, winner of the wrestling in 468, came from Opus, the capital of Eastern Locris, about 50 miles north-west of Pindar's home-city of Thebes. The closeness of the two cities may explain why Pindar says Opus is a city 'dear' to him (line 21), mentions its guest-friendship links with Thebes (line 83), and dwells on the victor and his past victories in unusual detail (lines 89–94, 111). Epharmostus was a prolific victor whose achievements lead Pindar to extol memorably the value of natural talent (line 100).

1 *Archilochus' song*: alluding to a refrain, attributed to the seventh-century lyric poet Archilochus, sung at Olympia shortly after the victory (cf. 'For he's a jolly good fellow, he's a jolly good fellow, he's a jolly good fellow and so say all of us') and contrasted by Pindar with his more elaborate ode performed back in the victor's home-city.

3 *Cronus's hill*: the hill of Cronus overlooked Olympia.

6 *scatter*: Pindar addresses himself.

9–10 *Pelops . . . Hippodameia's splendid dowry*: cf. *O.* 1.67–71.

12 *Pytho*: the Pythian games at Delphi, where Epharmostus had also won.

15–16 *Themis . . . Eunomia*: Justice and Good Order.

17 *Castalia*: spring at Delphi.

26 *the Graces*: see *O.* 14.

30 *Heracles*: Pindar selects stories about Heracles confronting Poseidon, Apollo, and Hades which (*a*) illustrate that he could only have done this with divine help, thus exemplifying lines 28–9 and implying that the same is true of the successes of Epharmostus too (cf. line 103 below), (*b*) advantageously offset the main myth that follows. Pindar quite often tongue-in-cheek says that he has chosen an inappropriate myth (cf. *P.* 11.38–40, *N.* 3.26–7).

41–2 *Protogeneia's city*: Opus. Pindar is probably inventing here, given his stress on the novelty of his myth (lines 48–9, 80). The story that follows is indebted to Hesiod's *Catalogue of Women* (esp. lines 45–6 ~ Hesiod Frag. 234 M-W). Although the genealogy is unclear at times, it serves to ennoble Epharmostus: he has Cronus as an ancestor (line 56) and his home-city Opus has connections with Elis (line 58) where the Olympic games were held.

45–6 *stones . . . people*: a pun in Greek.

55 *Iapetus'*: father of Prometheus and grandfather of Pyrrha and Deucalion.

58 *Epeians*: inhabitants of Elis, location of Olympia.

59 *Maenalus'*: mountain in Arcadia.

63–4 *name of his mother's father*: i.e. Opus.

65–6 *a man beyond telling in beauty and great deeds*: like Epharmostus himself (line 94).

70 *whose son*: Patroclus.

71 *Teuthras*: king of Mysia in Asia Minor, where the Greeks (Danaans) landed by mistake on the way to Troy and were attacked by Telephus, adopted son of Teuthras.

76 *Thetis' son*: Achilles. In what follows Pindar twists *Iliad* 16.89–90, where Achilles highlights Patroclus' weakness by warning him not to venture too far away; here the warning is taken to imply that Achilles cannot do without Patroclus' strength.

84 *Lampromachus'*: his name means 'Illustrious Fighter'; he seems to have been a citizen of Opus who was a *proxenos* of Thebes, i.e. looked after Theban interests in Opus by maintaining ties of guest-friendship.

84 *both men*: Lampromachus and Epharmostus.

86 *at the gates of Corinth*: in the Isthmian games again. These are probably further victories of Lampromachus, with the naming of Epharmostus in line 87 marking the beginning of the catalogue of victories of Epharmostus, probably eleven in all including the outstanding achievement of a victory in each of the big four (Olympic, Pythian, Nemean, and Isthmian).

96 *among the people of Parrhasia / at the festival for Lycaean Zeus*: in Arcadia, central Peloponnese.

98 *Pellana*: north-west Peloponnese.

98 *Iolaus'*: companion of Heracles; games in his honour were held in Pindar's home-city Thebes.

112 *Ajax, son of Ileus*: the 'Lesser', Locrian Ajax, honoured in Opus with a festival and altar. It seems that the ode was performed at the festival and Epharmostus' Olympic crown placed on the altar.

OLYMPIANS 10 AND 11

Both this ode and the much shorter *O*. 11 commemorate a victory in the boys' boxing by Hagesidamus from Epizephyrian (Western) Locri, a colony in south Italy of the Locrians of Opus in central Greece. The relationship between the two poems is uncertain, but Pindar probably composed *O*. 11 first and, to compensate for its brevity, perhaps caused by Hagesidamus' victory being in 476 the same year as Pindar was commissioned to compose *O*. 1–3, subsequently produced *O*. 10 when he had more time.

4 *Truth, daughter of Zeus*: Pindar invents genealogies of abstract deities to suit his *ad hoc* needs.

14 *Calliope*: one of the Muses; cf. *O*. 11.17–20 for the Epizephyrian Locrians as both warlike and cultured.

15 *Cycnus*: a son of Ares who constructed a temple to Apollo with the skulls of passers-by whom he had killed; different from the Cycnus of *O*. 2.82.

17 *Ilas*: probably Hagesidamus' coach, who perhaps helped Hagesidamus overcome an early setback in the boxing contest.

19 *Patroclus . . . Achilles*: if the allusion is to the beginning of *Iliad* 16 where Achilles spurs on Patroclus (see esp. line 126) and lends him his armour, then we must forget the fatal consequence.

25 *six altars*: cf. line 49 below and *O.* 5.5.

27–8 *Cteatus . . . Eurytus*: sons of Poseidon and allies of Augeas, king of Elis where the Epeians lived. He cheated Heracles of the payment promised for cleaning out his stables. Cleonae and Tiryns are cities near Argos, east of Elis. Heracles' achievements create a safe environment for the establishment of the Olympic games.

45 *Altis*: sacred grove of Zeus at Olympia.

55 *Time*: in the myth, the passage of time improves the situation, just as the timely production of this ode has helped Pindar (lines 7–12, 85).

66–70 *Midea . . . Tegea . . . Tiryns . . . Mantinea*: cities in central Peloponnese. Pindar is right in suggesting that the first Olympics were more of a local affair than the Panhellenic games they later became. The Olympics developed from a pre-existing cult of Zeus at Olympia. (The early Olympic victors listed in the *Chronicle* of Eusebius, third to fourth century AD, are local, later ones coming from further afield.)

85 *Dirce*: a spring in Pindar's home-city Thebes, a source of his poetic inspiration.

96 *Pierian daughters of Zeus*: the Muses.

105 *Ganymede*: loved by Zeus, he became the Olympians' immortal cupbearer and is a paradigm for the immortality conferred on the victor by Pindar's poetry.

OLYMPIAN 12

Ergoteles was an outstanding long-distance runner, winning twice at all four of the major games. This ode commemorates his first win at Olympia, in 472, after he had already won twice at the Pythian and Isthmian games, but was written before his Nemean victories and his second Olympic one since they are not mentioned. His second Olympic win is more likely to have been at the next Olympics in 468 than in 464 or later, as some have assumed, since long-distance runners rarely stay at the top for long; modern parallels for consecutive Olympic victories in long-distance running are Emil Zatopek, Waldemar Cierpinski, Lasse Viren, Abebe Bekela, and Haile Gebrselassie; Paavo Nurmi is the only man to become Olympic champion again in an event he first won two Olympics before. As the ode itself tells us (lines 13–19), Ergoteles came to Himera in Sicily after having to leave Cnossus in Crete.

1 *Zeus the Deliverer*: possibly an allusion to Hieron's defeat of Thrasydaeus, ruler of Acragas and son of Theron, which gave Himera freedom from control by Acragas towards the end of the 460s. More likely, Pindar simply means that Ergoteles enjoys in Himera freedom which he lacked in strife-ridden Cnossus.

15 *ingloriously*: Pindar means that Ergoteles would not have won athletics glory in Cnossus because of the unsettled political climate there.

19 *you bring fame*: after the games Ergoteles relaxes in, and thereby gives honour to, Himera's warm spring water; cf. *N.* 4.4–5.

OLYMPIAN 13

Xenophon of Corinth won both the stadion race and the pentathlon at the Olympics of 464. The feat is less surprising when one considers that the stadion race, besides being an event in its own right, was also part of the pentathlon. Xenophon must have been basically a sprinter who was also competent at the other disciplines of the pentathlon (long-jump, discus, javelin, wrestling); he inherited his running ability from his father, who was himself an outstanding runner, having been Olympic victor in a running event and won the stadion and diaulos (there and back) on the same day at the Pythian games (lines 35–7) besides numerous other victories elsewhere. Xenophon's whole family clan, the Oligaethidae, were fine athletes, amassing no fewer (according to Pindar) than sixty victories at the Nemean and Isthmian games. This background of supreme athletic success accounts for the cautionary nature of the myth: Xenophon should remember his mortality just as Bellerophon should have done with Pegasus (cf. lines 47–8, 'Each thing is attended by due measure, and to understand this brings the greatest profit'). A story in Athenaeus (second century AD) tells how after his victories Xenophon dedicated prostitutes to Aphrodite; Pindar composed another, light-hearted, poem for Xenophon celebrating them (Frag. 122).

4–5 *Poseidon's isthmus*: Corinth was situated by the Isthmus, the causeway connecting the Peloponnese with mainland Greece where the Isthmian games in honour of Poseidon were held.

8 *Themis*: divinely sanctioned law.

10 *Insolence . . . Excess*: Pindar implies that the praise that follows of all the victories of Xenophon's family might seem to some hubristic and excessive.

14 *sons of Aletes*: the Corinthians. Aletes was a legendary ruler of Corinth.

17 *Seasons*: the goddesses mentioned at lines 6–7, where they were goddesses of protection (Good Order, Justice, Peace). By a subtle use of the word 'many-flowered', Pindar now abandons their civic roles and regards them in a different way, as goddesses of opportunity who bring things to light.

19 *dithyramb*: hymn sung in competition honouring Dionysus; the winner may have been awarded an ox. Elsewhere Pindar says the dithyramb was invented in Thebes (Frag. 71) or Naxos (Frag. 115); he tailors his history to fit the occasion.

21 *twin kings of birds*: two eagles, probably an allusion to a temple's triangular (wing-shaped) twin pediments.

40 *Hellotian*: games in Corinth for Athena Hellotis. Competitors ran holding torches.

40 *Poseidon's festival*: the Isthmian games.

41 *Ptoeodorus*: Thessalus' father, so Xenophon's grandfather; Terpsias and Eritimus were probably Thessalus' uncle and cousin.

44 *lion's haunts*: the Nemean games.

52 *Sisyphus*: legendary king of Corinth and trickster (cf. *Iliad* 6.152–4).

53 *Medea*: daughter of Aeetes, a king of Corinth according to the eighth-century epic poet Eumelus (Frags. 2–3 Davies), whom Pindar may be following here. Usually he is king of Colchis, from where Medea fled to Corinth with Jason after helping him get the golden fleece.

58 *Atreus' dear sons*: Agamemnon and Menelaus.

60 *Glaucus*: Pindar resumes the mention of Sisyphus, who was the son of Aeolus and grandfather of Bellerophon, Glaucus' father according to Pindar here. Glaucus' connection with Lycia comes from Bellerophon's being sent there to escape a false accusation of rape. Pindar's story of Bellerophon is based on the extended treatment in the *Iliad* within Glaucus' speech to Diomedes (*Iliad* 6.145–211), though his genealogy of the descendants of Aeolus differs in some details from that in the *Iliad*, perhaps because he is using also a different version, perhaps through idiosyncratic variation.

61 *Peirene's*: fountain in Corinth, referred to again in 'the spring' below.

67 *waking vision*: cf. *O.* 1.73–4, *O.* 6.61–2.

68 *charmer of horses*: the bit, that 'charms' horses.

69 *father the horse-tamer*: Poseidon.

75 *Coeranus' son*: Polyidus, a seer related to famous prophetic Melampus clan.

78 *spirit-taming gold*: i.e. the bit.

90 *Solymi*: a tribe of warriors in Asia Minor.

91 *his fate*: Bellerophon tried to ride Pegasus to Olympus, but was struck down by Zeus and ended up wandering lonely and sad over the 'Land of Wandering' (*Iliad* 6.200–2; cf. *I.* 7.44–7). Pegasus had a happier end, conveying to Zeus his thunder and lightning on Olympus (Hesiod, *Theogony* 285–6).

106 *Enyalius*: Ares. Perhaps Pindar is alluding to the race in armour.

108 *the Lycaean*: Zeus.

109 *precinct of the Aeacids*: Aegina.

114 *Come, swim out*: Pindar addresses himself, using a metaphor appropriate to Corinth which was by the sea.

OLYMPIAN 14

An odd epinician, of uncertain date, since no indication is given in the ode of which event the victor Asopichus had won. It is mainly a hymn to the Graces (Aglaia=Radiance, Euphrosyne=Good Cheer, Thalia=Festivity, lines 13–15), specially worshipped at the victor's home-city of Orchomenus in

Boeotia, about 30 miles north-west of Pindar's Thebes. The ode reveals (lines 5–7) how important Pindar thought divine help was for any type of human success.

1 *Cephisus*: a river near Orchomenus.

4 *Minyans*: descendants of the legendary Minyas, whose son was called Orchomenus and founded the eponymous Boeotian city. Pausanias (9.36.6) says that the people of Boeotian Orchomenus continued to be called Minyans to distinguish them from people of another Orchomenus in Arcadia.

17 *Lydian mode*: see note on *O.* 5.19.

20–1 *house of Persephone*: the Underworld. Pindar cleverly finds a way of including the victor's dead father: the victory celebration will reverberate even to the house of the dead.

PYTHIAN 1

Although nominally an epinician in honour of the victory in the chariot race by Hieron, tyrant of Syracuse, in 470 at the Pythian games (see lines 32–40), this ode is more concerned with the political implications of Hieron's founding of the city of Aetna (formerly Catana) in 476/5 and his military achievements. At the time the ode was written, Hieron was ill (suffering from dysury, or difficulty in passing urine, according to Aristotle cited at Sch. *P.* 1.89a), a condition alluded to in the comparison with Philoctetes (lines 50–1). He was afflicted by this condition for a number of years (cf. headnote to *P.* 3), and died in 466. The last triad of both this ode and *P.* 2 is devoted to moral and political advice to Hieron: such a powerful tyrant, with the potential to do both good and bad, will have needed it and Pindar was confident enough to give it. Contrast *O.* 1, probably composed before *P.* 1 and 2, which presents Hieron as a man of culture (*O.* 1.13–17) and lacks the overtly didactic final triad.

12 *Leto's son*: Apollo.

14 *Pierians*: Muses, who had a home at Pieria, a region north of Mt. Olympus.

17 *Typhos*: his overthrow by Zeus is described by Hesiod (*Theogony* 820–80), but Pindar's specification of the location of his imprisonment seems to be his invention to make the episode relevant to Hieron, who defeated the Etruscans off Cumae in 474, was tyrant of Syracuse, and had recently founded Aetna. Cumae is near Naples, about 200 miles north of Sicily. So Typhos lies in a large area under the Tyrrhenian Sea.

30 *namesake city*: Aetna.

39 *Phoebus*: Apollo, the god in whose honour the Pythian games were held. Pindar mentions three of his cult centres.

42 *that famous man*: Hieron.

47 *battles*: besides defeating the Etruscans at Cumae, Hieron had helped his brother Gelon of Syracuse with Theron of Acragas to defeat a huge Carthaginian invading force (the Phoenician battle-cry mentioned

in line 72 below) led by Hamilcar at Himera in 480; but his illness meant he had to be carried in a litter (Sch. *P.* 1.89b, 97), hence the analogy with Philoctetes, son of Poeas, who helped the Greeks capture Troy despite a poisoned foot which had caused him to be abandoned on the island of Lemnos. He was later cured, as Pindar hopes Hieron will be.

58 *Deinomenes'*: Hieron's son, whom Hieron appointed ruler of the newly founded city of Aetna; he inherited his name from his grandfather (mentioned in line 79).

62–6 *according to the ordinances of Hyllus' rule*: Pindar is here saying that Hieron has founded his new city of Aetna in accordance with good old Greek values. The occupation of the Peloponnese by Heracles' descendants was a story designed to explain the origins of the rise to power of Dorian western Greek city-states. Pindar here says that they came from northern Greece (the Pindus mountains in Thessaly) and settled in Sparta. He singles out two Dorians, Hyllus, Heracles' son, and Pamphylus, a son of Aegimius, another descendant (cf. *I.* 9.1–4, a fragment of an *Isthmian* ode not included in this edition but translated in the Loeb edition of Pindar, ii. 217–19). Sparta is alluded to by the references to Mt. Taygetus and Amyclae (an early settlement near Sparta where Castor and Polydeuces, the sons of Tyndareus, were worshipped). Cf. note to *I.* 7.12–15.

67 *Amenas*: river by Aetna.

76–7 *Salamis . . . the battles before Cithaeron*: Pindar alludes to two major battles in the Persian Wars against Xerxes. In late 480 the Greeks (principally the Athenians) defeated the Persians, or 'Medes', off the island of Salamis near Athens; the Persians withdrew and in the summer of the following year were decisively beaten (this time principally by the Spartans) at Plataea near Thebes and Mt. Cithaeron.

81 *If you should speak . . . occasion*: what follows reminds us that there is more to Pindar's epinicians than mere praise. Poets were traditionally wise repositories of truth, so their advice, even if as here expressed bluntly, would have been respected, indeed sought, by rulers.

94–6 *Croesus . . . Phalaris*: examples of good and bad rulers, Croesus a friendly, wealthy and generous king of Lydia (*c.*560–546), Phalaris a monstrously cruel tyrant of Acragas (*c.*570–549) who roasted his enemies alive in a bronze bull.

PYTHIAN 2

The date and venue of the victory commemorated in this ode are not known; it may not even be for a Pythian victory. The ode illustrates the flexibility of the epinician genre, which could range from a short poem focusing almost exclusively on athletics (e.g. *N.* 2), to a poem like the present one, of typical length but having very little to do with athletics or athletics victories (cf. *P.* 3), or (an extreme case) to the massive *P.* 4.

2 *sanctuary of Ares*: alluding to unspecified military campaigns of Hieron; cf. lines 19, 65, 87.

6 *Ortygia*: see note to *O.* 6.92.

7 *river-goddess Artemis*: alluding to the pursuit by the river Alpheus of the nymph Arethusa to Ortygia where she emerged as a spring and there was a cult of Artemis (the 'maiden goddess' of line 9). Cf. *N.* 1.1–3.

12 *the wide-ruling god, the trident-holder*: Poseidon, god of horses.

15 *Cinyras*: a wealthy and hospitable king of Cyprus, who gave Agamemnon a breastplate as a token of friendship (*Iliad* 11.19–23).

18–19 *maiden of Western Locri*: Pindar seems to mean, obscurely, that as a result of Hieron's (unspecified) military help, the colony of Western Locri in south Italy (see headnote to *O.* 10) was rendered safe and in return a chorus of girls sang outdoors in his honour.

21 *Ixion*: in contrast to Cinyras he not only lacked gratitude but was arrogant and hubristic: besides attempting to rape Hera, instead of paying his father-in-law for the hand of his daughter he lured him to his death in a hidden pit of fire. Punished by Zeus for his crimes, he provides a lesson for Hieron.

44 *Centaurus*: Pindar derives the name from the Greek for 'goad' and 'air'.

45 *Magnesia*: near Thessaly and Mt. Pelion in northern Greece.

55 *Archilochus*: seventh-century lyric poet who, according to Pindar, became wealthy from his ungracious invective, which is said to have driven some of his victims even to suicide.

67–9 *Phoenician merchandise . . . song of Castor*: Pindar here somewhat obscurely apparently splits up *P.* 2 into two parts. The first part (the first three triads), like merchandise, is for widespread public consumption. The second part (the last triad) is more for Hieron's personal reflection. 'Aeolian strings' is a musical metaphor, individuating the Castor-song, whose meaning is lost to us.

73 *Rhadamanthys*: a proverbially wise judge of the souls of the dead in the Underworld. Pindar means here 'be of mature judgement and see things as they really are'.

PYTHIAN 3

This is a poem consoling Hieron for his chronic illness (see headnote to *P.* 1), not an epinician though classified as one in antiquity because it mentions the past Pythian victories of Hieron by his horse Pherenicus in the single-horse race (lines 73–4). These victories were in 482 and 478 (*P.* 3 Inscr. a). Since Pindar mentions them as the crowning moments of Hieron's athletics career, and does not recall any of his even more illustrious Olympic victories (476, 472, 468), it seems probable that the poem was composed around 477 before the Olympic victories had taken place. It focuses on the futility of yearning for the impossible.

1 *Chiron*: a kindly and wise centaur who educated a number of heroes; cf. *N*. 3.53—5.

8 *daughter of Phlegyas*: Coronis (named at line 25).

19 *evening songs*: cf. *P.* 11.10.

28 *Loxias*: Apollo.

34 *Lacereia . . . Boebias*: place and lake in north-east Thessaly, near where Chiron lived.

61 *my soul*: Pindar speaks to himself here, though what he says is applicable to Hieron too.

67 *a son of Leto's child or of his father*: Asclepius (son of Apollo, whose mother was Leto) or Apollo himself (son of Zeus); both were healers.

69 *Arethusa*: see note to *P.* 2.7.

74 *Cirrha*: a port on the plain south of Delphi. The plain was the venue for the equestrian events in the Pythian games.

78 *the Mother . . . Pan*: Pindar associates the Mother Goddess (probably Rhea, mother of Zeus) with Pan (a god of the countryside) in another poem, of which only two fragments survive; see Frag. 95.1—3: 'O Pan . . . companion of the Great Mother.' Why Pindar specifies these two divinities here in *Pythian 3* is not clear, perhaps Rhea as a saviour goddess (she saved Zeus from his father Cronus) and Pan as a god of countryside caves (relevant to Chiron). He seems to mean it is more beneficial for him not to travel to Sicily but to pray for divine help for Hieron. For a similarly obscure claim to domestic religiosity, cf. *P.* 8.58—60.

81 *for every blessing . . . a double grief*: at *Iliad* 24.527—33 Homer says Zeus has two jars, one of good things, one of bad, and gives to mortals either only from the latter or (at best) a mixture.

87—8 *Peleus . . . Cadmus*: Peleus married Thetis on Mt. Pelion; their only son, Achilles, died in the Trojan War. Cadmus and Harmonia were married in Thebes; three of their four daughters (Ino, Autonoë, Agave) went mad and/or killed/lost their sons; the fourth, Thyone (Semele), was killed by Zeus when he came to her as a thunderbolt when she was pregnant with Dionysus.

112 *Nestor and Lycian Sarpedon*: the poet Homer made these two heroes famous; similarly, Pindar's poetry can give fame.

PYTHIANS 4 AND 5

P. 4 and 5 are both for Arcesilas IV, king of Cyrene, a Greek colony in Libya, north Africa, in celebration of Arcesilas' victory in the chariot race in 462. *P.* 4 is abnormally long because it combines material relevant to Arcesilas as king of Cyrene and descendant of its founder Battus with a plea by Pindar that Arcesilas recall from exile Damophilus, Pindar's friend whom the king had exiled from Cyrene. Lines 263–99 explicitly urge the king to recall him, but within the long myth in the earlier part of the poem, especially the part about Jason's reclaiming of his kingdom from the usurper Pelias, the themes of *xenia* (guest-friendship), one's rightful dues, and courtesy surface a number of times: lines 29–31, 104–5, 127–31, 136–7, 159–60 (see note on 'Phrixus'); Pindar thereby indirectly hints to Arcesilas how he should treat Damophilus. In addition, he describes the expedition of the Argonauts and Jason's accomplishment of his goals in language resonant of competition in the games (see lines 185–6, 240), so making them relevant to Arcesilas.

The myth itself is somewhat complicatedly presented: first, the Delphic oracle prophesies that Battus will colonize Libya from the island of Thera (a colony of Sparta) and thereby fulfil seventeen generations later a prophecy Medea once gave to the Argonauts (lines 4–12); then comes Medea's prophecy itself in which she tells how a god in the guise of a man gave to Euphamus, one of the Argonauts, a clod of earth from Libya; this clod was lost overboard at Thera, and consequently delayed the colonization of Libya from Thera until seventeen generations later when Battus, a descendant of Euphamus, himself fulfilling a Delphic oracle, sailed from Thera to Libya as a cure for his stammer and became the founder of Cyrene (lines 13–56). So far, Pindar has explained Arcesilas' heroic descent from Euphamus, even though, more immediately, he was eighth in line after Battus (see line 65) who became king *c*.630 BC, and has thereby glorified Arcesilas' ancestry (cf. Herodotus 4.150–9). During a pause in the mythologizing Pindar mentions in one word Arcesilas' chariot victory (line 67), and then launches in epic style into the main myth of the ode, Jason and the Argonauts (lines 69–262), focusing (lines 71–167) on Jason's meeting with Pelias, the usurper of his father's kingdom, and the expedition of the Argonauts to recover the golden fleece as ordered by Pelias (lines 168–246). Pindar then links the Argonauts with Arcesilas by telling how after the expedition the Argonauts slept with the women of the isle of Lemnos, and from Euphamus' family Arcesilas is descended (lines 247–62). One can imagine that, if the Damophilus problem had not occurred, Pindar might have restricted the mythical episode to the recovery of the golden fleece, which would have kept the ode to normal length.

P. 5 is a more regular ode, though unusual inasmuch as Pindar (compensating for the virtual absence of athletics in *P.* 4) goes into some detail about the athletics victory itself, telling us that the victorious chariot remained intact when forty other charioteers fell (lines 49–51) and that the race was twelve laps long (line 33). The ode seems to have been performed in Cyrene at the Carnea, a Dorian festival honouring Apollo (lines 22–3, 79–80).

PYTHIAN 4

3 *Leto's children*: Apollo, in whose honour the Pythian games were held, and his twin sister Artemis.

4 *golden eagles*: the Delphic oracle functioned through the Pythian priestess who prophesied sitting near two gold statues of eagles, the bird of Zeus (cf. *P.* 1.6–10).

holy island . . . city of fine chariots: Thera, modern Santorini, and Cyrene, a colony dispatched from Thera, with an allusion to Arcesilas' chariot victory.

14 *daughter of Epaphus*: Libya.

16 *Zeus Ammon*: Ammon (in Egyptian, Amun) was the name of the chief Egyptian god, who was identified with Zeus (cf. Pindar, Frag. 36, 'Ammon, lord of Olympus', the beginning of a Hymn to Ammon) and famous for his oracle at Siwa.

20 *Lake Tritonis'*: in Libya; the implication is that Euphamus received the clod from a Triton, half-fish and half-man, disguised as a man.

33 *Holder / and Shaker of the Earth*: Poseidon.

42 *this island*: Thera (cf. lines 51–2 below). The point of this part of the story is that, because the clod of Libyan soil was washed back to Thera, therefore Thera was destined to found later a colony in Libya: the foundation of the colony would, as it were, be a rightful return of Libyan soil to Libya. So the colonization of Libya from Thera by Battus (the 'hero' of line 52, and 'son of Polymnastus' in line 59) is legitimized. Cyrene's Spartan origins are touched on several times in *P.* 4 and 5: here, lines 257–8, *P.* 5.72–6; the colony thereby has connections with the Dorians, who were according to popular tradition early settlers in Sparta and whose 'good old' values Pindar approved of (cf. note to *O.* 1.17). Underlying the 'lost clod' story may be the failure of the Spartan colonist Dorieus to colonize Libya in the early fifth century (cf. Herodotus 5.42).

44 *Taenarus*: in Laconia (cf. line 49); 'it' refers to the clod. For Cephisus, see note to *O.* 14.1.

50 *foreign women*: the women of Lemnos (cf. lines 252–7).

55 *a journey to Pytho's temple*: to find a cure for his stammer (cf. line 63 and Herodotus 4.154–9).

60 *Delphic bee*: Pythian priestess.

69 *Minyans*: Argonauts.

71 *Pelias*: unlawful king of Iolcus (line 77), descendant (like Jason) of Aeolus (line 108) and son of Tyro (line 136).

74 *navel-stone*: Delphi, situated at the centre of mother earth.

80 *Magnesian*: from Magnesia in Thessaly, northern Greece, where the wild centaurs lived (cf. *P.* 2.45, *P.* 3.45).

87–8 *Aphrodite's husband*: Ares.

89–90 *Otus . . . Ephialtes . . . Tityus*: giants; cf. *Iliad* 5.385–6; *Odyssey* 11.307–20, 576–81.

92 *pleasures*: Tityus was killed by Artemis while attempting to rape her mother Leto.

102 *teachings of Chiron*: cf. *N*. 3.53–4. Chariclo and Philyra were Chiron's wife and mother. Jason (in Greek the name suggests 'healer') was brought up among women; his father was Aeson (line 118), son of Tyro (line 136).

125–6 *Pheres . . . Amythaon . . . Admetus . . . Melampus*: Pheres was father of Admetus, Amythaon father of Melampus.

142–3 *Cretheus and reckless Salmoneus*: sons of Aeolus and his wife; Salmoneus pretended to be Zeus, who killed him for his arrogance.

160 *Phrixus*: 'Pindar is unique here too, bidding Jason recall from Aea not just the fleece but also the soul of Phrixus because the gods of the Underworld were angry, other writers saying he was sent to retrieve only the fleece' (Sch. 281a); so the voyage of the Argonauts is partly motivated by religious duty. Phrixus escaped his wicked stepmother Ino by flying on the back of a ram with golden fleece to Colchis, on the Black Sea, where he died; he came from Thessaly, to where his dead body needed to be returned and where he was buried.

163 *Castalia*: spring at Delphi.

171 *three sons*: Heracles, and Castor and Polydeuces.

172–3 *two long-haired men*: sons of Poseidon, the Earthshaker, Euphamus from Taenarus and Periclymenus from Pylos.

180 *Pangaeon*: mountain in Thrace.

203 *Inhospitable Sea*: Black Sea.

208–9 *Clashing Rocks*: the Symplegades, which guarded the entrance to the Black Sea by clashing together if a ship approached; cf. *Odyssey* 12.61–72.

211 *Phasis*: river.

241 *son of Helios*: Aeetes, father of Medea and king of Colchis.

242 *Phrixus' knives*: after his escape Phrixus had sacrificed the ram and skinned it to obtain the fleece.

258–9 *island of Calliste*: Thera. Pindar returns to the theme of lines 50–3.

263 *Learn now the wisdom of Oedipus*: in what follows Pindar urges Arcesilas to recall Damophilus. Oedipus is mentioned because he was wise enough to solve the riddle of the Sphinx and, like Damophilus, he was forced into exile.

270 *Paean*: appropriate both as the god of healing and as equivalent to Apollo who, as god presiding over the Pythian games, gave a glorious victory to Arcesilas.

277 *among Homer's sayings*: *Iliad* 15.207, 'This too is good, when a messenger knows what is right'.

294 *Apollo's spring*: in Cyrene.

299 *in Thebes*: as guest of Pindar, with whom Damophilus evidently stayed after his exile from Cyrene. The final word of the ode ('guest-friendship') is the central theme of the ode: Pindar leaves Arcesilas with an unequivocal reminder of his obligations towards Damophilus.

PYTHIAN 5

See headnote to *P.* 4.

9 *Castor*: famous as a charioteer; cf. *I.* 1.17.

10 *rain*: an allusion to political unrest.

15–19 *first, because you are a king . . . judgement*: text and sense are uncertain.

26 *Carrhotus*: Arcesilas' charioteer, son of Alexibias (line 45).

27–8 *he did not bring with him . . . Hindsight*: i.e. because he won he did not have to make any excuses for losing.

37 *Crisa*: same as Cirrha (*P.* 3.74).

40 *statue*: we know nothing else about this.

49–50 *forty charioteers fell*: chariot racing was dangerous (analogous to modern Formula One motor-car racing), so the wealthy and eminent victors did not normally take part themselves but employed charioteers.

57–8 *Even deep-roaring lions*: Pindar does not mention, but perhaps knew, the undignified story (Pausanias 10.15.7) that Battus, whose name means 'stammerer', was cured of his stammer when he encountered a lion in Cyrene and cried out in fear. In homage to Battus, Pindar reverses the roles and makes the lions run away afraid.

62 *oracles*: cf. *P.* 4.59–63.

71–2 *mighty sons of Heracles and of Aegimius*: see note to *P.* 1.62–6. Settlements were regularly established in obedience to an oracle, which thereby provided divine sanction.

72–80 *my cherished glory . . . we honour*: Pindar adopts the rhetorical strategy of identifying himself with the Cyreneans, effecting a bond between poet, chorus, and audience.

83 *the sons of Antenor*: cf. e.g. *Iliad* 3.203–24. Pindar thereby gives the Cyreneans another strand to their noble background.

83 *with Helen*: alluding to the story that during the Trojan War Antenor had advised the return of Helen to the Greeks.

87 *Aristoteles*: original name of Battus, the latter being a nickname.

94–5 *among men . . . a hero*: colonists (such as Battus) along with great athletes (e.g. Cleomedes, Pausanias 6.9.8) and other distinguished men sometimes achieved after their death an elevated status as a hero, along with special hero-worship.

120–1 *stormy blasts of autumn winds*: another political metaphor for 'revolution' (cf. line 10 and note). Arcesilas was assassinated in a democratic coup some time after the date of *P.* 11 (Herodotus 4.167).

PYTHIAN 6

P. 6 and *P.* 12, also for a victor from Acragas, were composed for victories in 490 and, after *P.* 10, are Pindar's earliest surviving odes; all three are by

Pindaric standards relatively straightforward compared to the complexities of some later ones. *P.* 6 celebrates a chariot victory of Xenocrates, a member of the Emmenidae clan (line 5) and brother of Theron, tyrant of Acragas, whose chariot victories Pindar was to celebrate in *O.* 2 and 3, but is devoted as much to his son Thrasybulus, whom Pindar addresses in two other poems also (*I.* 2 and Frag. 124ab). Hence the mythical parallel with Antilochus and his father Nestor (lines 29–43); if Thrasybulus helped his father by driving the chariot to victory, then the mention of Antilochus helping his father's chariot is even more apt.

1 *Aphrodite . . . Graces*: Pindar gives the poem an erotic touch, foreshadowing the prominence in it of the young man Thrasybulus.

22 *Philyra's son*: the centaur Chiron who brought up Achilles. Pindar next (lines 23–7) draws from *The Precepts of Chiron*, a didactic poem by Hesiod in which Chiron gives moral advice to Achilles, and in what follows about Antilochus saving Nestor from Memnon, the Ethiopian son of the dawn, probably from the *Aethiopis*, an epic poem from a time later than Homer.

33–4 *He was shaking his mighty spear*: Memnon.

PYTHIAN 7

This, one of Pindar's shortest odes, celebrates a victory in the chariot race of 486 by Megacles, a member of the famous and rich Alcmaeonidae family of Athens, prominent in Athenian politics during the seventh to fifth centuries. Its members included Alcmaeon, the victor's great-grandfather, whom Croesus allowed to stuff himself with as much gold as he could carry (Herodotus 6.125), Cleisthenes, the victor's uncle, who introduced democratic reforms into Athens (splitting it up into demes and instituting ostracism), Pericles, a nephew, and Alcibiades, a grandson. Suitably for a Pythian ode, Pindar singles out (lines 10–11) the family's rebuilding of the temple of Apollo at Delphi in 548 (cf. Herodotus 5.62). The family (like the Sicilian tyrants) had numerous successes in equestrian events at the games (lines 13–17), and these would have boosted their political prestige still further: sport had a political dimension then as now. The last lines (lines 18–21) probably allude to Megacles' being in exile at the time of the poem's composition, a victim of ostracism.

10 *Erechtheus'*: legendary early king of Athens.

PYTHIAN 8

A wistful ode, Pindar's latest surviving one, for Aristomenes, winner in the boys' wrestling in 446. The invocation of 'Concord' at the beginning and the 'freeborn voyage' at the end have political resonances and seem to allude to harsh treatment by Athens towards Aegina in the 450s.

12 *Porphyrion*: king of the Giants.

16 *Typhos*: see *P*. 1.15–28.

19–20 *Xenarces' son*: Aristomenes.

36 *Theognetus*: also a victor in the boys' wrestling (Pausanias 6.9.1).

39 *Oecles' son*: Amphiaraus (line 56). The Epigoni (line 42) were the sons
of the Seven against Thebes; unlike their fathers, they successfully
attacked Thebes. But whereas in the first attack Adrastus, alone of the
Seven, survived, in the second attack his son alone died (lines 52–3).
Alcman was Amphiaraus' son, and the main point of the story is that
he inherited his father's prowess just as the victor Aristomenes
follows in his ancestors' footsteps.

55 *streets of Abas*: Argos, from where the Seven and the Epigoni came.

56–60 *and I too am glad to throw garlands at Alcman . . . hereditary skills*:
a difficult passage. It seems best to interpret Pindar as (*a*) adopting the
rhetorical strategy of representing himself as the victor (cf. note to
N. 7.85), (*b*) speaking metaphorically, (*c*) suggesting an association
between Alcman and the victor: I (Pindar on behalf of the victor) con-
gratulate Alcman and praise him in song because, caring for me as if
he were my neighbour and guardian, he met me (associated himself
with me) as I was on my way to the famous navel of the earth (Delphi,
where the Pythian games were held) and used his inherited prophetic
skills (foretold my victory by means of inherited skill, i.e. his skill in
prophesying inherited from his father the prophet Amphiaraus
revealed the likelihood of Aristomenes' victory since the latter came
from a family of victorious athletes). In sum, the passage means that
Alcman provides a good heroic example for the victor because he
shows the power of inherited ability.

61 *Far-shooter*: Apollo.

66 *pentathlon*: wrestling was part of the pentathlon, so, if he was good at
boxing too and competent at one of the other disciplines (sprint,
javelin, discus) it is not surprising Aristomenes could be a victor in
the pentathlon; in ancient Greek athletics the pool of talented athletes
was smaller than nowadays, so we hear of several athletes victorious at
even the major games in dissimilar events (e.g. Theagenes of Thasos,
boxer, pancratiast, and long-distance runner, Pausanias 6.11.5). The
scholia here tell us that he won the pentathlon at the Delphinia games
to Apollo and Artemis on Aegina, minor games where it would be
even easier for a wrestler to win the pentathlon.

83–4 *no homeward way . . . happy as yours*: for the misery of the defeated,
cf. *O*. 8.67–9 and note.

99–100 *Zeus . . . Aeacus . . . Peleus . . . Telamon . . . Achilles*: father, son,
grandsons, great-grandson. Zeus and the nymph Aegina, eponymous
heroine of the island, were ancestors of the great Aeacid family whose
prowess Pindar regularly associates with the victorious athletes from
Aegina.

PYTHIAN 9

The race in armour was a run to the end and back in the stadium. Competitors carried a large hoplite shield (see line 1) and wore a helmet (and sometimes greaves too), and clashed with their shields as they ran (see *I.* 1.23). The event shows the influence of the military on Greek athletics. An analogous modern race is the steeplechase, where obstacles to easy running are deliberately incorporated; long-jumping with weights is another event where the effort needed to perform has been increased by the need to carry extra equipment. Telesicrates, from Cyrene (see headnote to *P.* 4 and 5), won the event in 474. Pindar tells us (lines 97–103) how admired he was by women who had seen him compete. The ode is dominated by a humorous and mildly erotic myth about Apollo's desire for the eponymous heroine Cyrene, and is followed by a shorter myth with a marital theme. The tone is thus different from the serious didactic in Pindar's odes for the Sicilian tyrants (*O.* 1–3, *P.* 1–3), for example.

5 *son of Leto*: Apollo, the 'Delian guest' of line 10.

5 *Pelion's*: a mountain in Thessaly.

8 *third root*: Europe, Asia, and Africa are imagined as constituting the world, each part descending like a root into the ground.

13–14 *Hypseus . . . king of the haughty Lapiths*: the wild heroine Cyrene is naturally daughter of a Lapith, a wild and warlike people most famous for their fight with the Centaurs (depicted on the Parthenon Frieze and west pediment of the Temple of Zeus at Olympia). The genealogy and story that follow are probably derived from Hesiod's epic *Catalogue of Women* (see. Sch. *P.* 9.6a). Pindus and Peneus are a Thessalian mountain and river, here inserted into the family tree.

53 *Zeus' magnificent garden*: Libya, alluding to its fertility (cf. lines 6a–7) and the oracle of Zeus Ammon (see note to *P.* 4.16).

54–5 *island people*: those from Thera led by Battus (see *P.* 4.6–9).

65 *Agreus and Nomius*: Hunter and Shepherd. The child, Aristaeus, will be worshipped as a local Greek god, either as Apollo the Hunter/Shepherd or as Zeus Aristaeus.

71–2 *son of Carneiadas*: names beginning 'Carn-' were common in Cyrene because of the cult there of Apollo Carneias (see headnote to *P.* 4 and 5, last paragraph).

79 *Iolaus*: nephew and companion of Heracles, son of Heracles' twin brother Iphicles, and grandson of Amphitryon/Zeus and Alcmene. He appropriately rose from the dead to kill king Eurystheus, who had set Heracles twelve labours and was menacing Heracles' children. The 'Sown Men' are the Thebans, sown from the dragon's teeth by Thebes' founder Cadmus. The excursus on Iolaus is prompted by the praise of 'appropriateness' (line 78) and enables Pindar to bring in his favourite hero, Heracles.

88 *Dirce*: spring at Thebes from where Pindar drew his inspiration.

91 *Nisus*: king of Megara. Telesicrates had been victorious at games here and on Aegina.

94 *Old Man of the Sea*: Nereus, a wise prophet and god.

98–101 *Pallas'* . . . *Olympian* . . . *Earth*: local games at Cyrene, which (like the big Olympics) unmarried women could attend.

106 *Irasa*: 'the fairest place in Libya' (Herodotus 4.158).

106 *Antaeus*: usually an unpleasant giant who lived in Libya (cf. *I.* 4.52–5); here he is a fairly normal father.

112 *Danaus*: grandson of the heroine Libya. His fifty daughters (the Danaids), forced to marry the fifty sons of his brother Aegyptus, fled to Argos and all except two killed their husbands. Pindar seems to have invented, to fit into the epinician context, the way in which the remaining forty-eight found new husbands. The story is relevant to Telesicrates, not only because Alexidamus is one of his ancestors (line 105) and a fast runner, but also because as a victorious athlete his marriage (whenever it comes) will be a glorious occasion (cf. *P.* 10.59).

PYTHIAN 10

Pindar's earliest surviving ode (498), for Hippocleas, a winner in the boys' diaulos, a run to the end of the stadium and back. He belonged to the aristocratic Aleuadae family (line 5), led by Thorax (line 64) from Larissa in Thessaly. The myth about Perseus' journey to the blessed Hyperboreans illustrates clearly how Pindar thought a victor in the games had performed a heroic achievement and reached an elevated status but should nevertheless be aware of his mortality.

1–2 *Lacedaemon* . . . *Thessaly*: the mention of the two together may have been influenced by their being political allies at the time of composition.

4 *Pelinna*: the victor's home-town.

14 *armour of Ares*: i.e. the race in armour.

16 *Phricias*: probably Hippocleas' father.

30 *Hyperboreans*: a fantastic people of the far north who live in a blessed condition, analogous to that of the victor, but can never really be reached by human beings, thus underlining the special status of the victor and his limitations. The fact that Perseus went to them and then returned alludes to the victor's bliss being ephemeral, like Pelops' ascent to Olympus and return to earth in *O.* 1.

36 *upright arrogance*: an allusion to the donkeys' sexual excitement.

45 *Danae's son*: Perseus. The story is told more fully at *P.* 12.11–17.

55–6 *Ephyra* . . . *Peneius*: a place and river in Thessaly.

PYTHIAN 11

For Thrasydaeus, a Theban, probably commemorating a victory in the boys' stadion race in 474. The myth, a mini-*Oresteia*, is relevant to Thrasydaeus because it concerns a young man who renewed his father's honour (lines 41–8) and draws attention to the danger inherent in success (lines 29–30). The opening lines could suggest that the ode was performed to accompany a celebratory procession to the shrine of Apollo Ismenius at Thebes, but one must be cautious about taking them literally (cf. *N.* 9.1–3).

1–4 *Semele . . . Ino . . . mother of Heracles . . . Melia's*: local Theban heroines; Semele and Ino were daughters of Cadmus and Harmonia. The mother of Heracles was Alcmene. Melia was a daughter of Ocean.

6 *Ismenion*: the oracle of Apollo Ismenius at Thebes (cf. Herodotus 8.134).

9 *Themis*: a goddess of justice, who presided over Delphi before Apollo.

15–16 *Pylades, guest-friend of Laconian Orestes*: Strophius, father of Pylades, was king of Phocis, the district where Delphi and the Pythian games were situated. Orestes was taken away from his murderous mother Clytaemestra and her lover Aegisthus by his nurse Arsinoe (line 17) and given to Strophius (line 35) to bring up safely along with his own son. Orestes is 'Laconian', i.e. Spartan, because Pindar follows Stesichorus (*PMG* 216), who like Aeschylus wrote an *Oresteia*, in placing Agamemnon's palace not (as in Homer) in Mycenae, which had become unimportant by Pindar's day, but at Amyclae (line 32) in Laconia.

21 *Acheron's*: river of the Underworld.

22 *Euripus*: where the Greek fleet gathered before sailing to Troy.

38 *My friends*: not an apology for the myth having been irrelevant to the victor (which it is not), but an amusing way of suggesting the importance of the glorious athletics victories.

60–2 *Iolaus . . . Castor . . . Polydeuces*: like the victor they are famous in song so will not be forgotten. For the latter two, cf. *N.* 10.55–90; they had a shrine at Therapne, near Sparta.

PYTHIAN 12

The Pythian games were held in honour of Apollo, god of music, and included a number of musical competitions: singing to the cithara, cithara-playing, and pipe-playing. The pipe, or *aulos*, was played in pairs. Midas of Acragas won the pipe-playing in 490, and in this ode Pindar explains in a myth how the instrument acquired its wide range of expressive sound ('melody of many heads', line 23).

3 *Acragas*: a river, with the same name as the city.

11 *Perseus*: see *P.* 10.46–8.

11 *one of the three sisters*: Medusa (line 16), one of the sisters, along with Euryale (line 20) and Stheno, who were the Gorgons; they and the Graeae, the three

old women with one eye between them who told Perseus the way to the Gorgons, were all daughters of Phorcus.

12 *Seriphus*: about 60 miles south-east of Athens.

14 *Polydectes*: king of Seriphos.

14 *his mother*: Danae.

17 *liquid stream of gold*: Zeus came to Danae in a shower of gold.

26–7 *Cephisis' precinct / beside the city of the Graces*: Orchomenus, in Boeotia, was by the river Cephisus, whose daughter was Cephisis; cf. *O*. 14.1–4.

NEMEAN 1

N. 1 is memorable for its account of Heracles strangling the snakes sent against him by Hera when he was a baby. His successes gained through natural strength are analogous to those of the victor, Chromius, son of Hagesidamus (line 29), who had won in the chariot race and was a Syracusan general serving under Hieron.

2 *Ortygia*: see *O*. 6.92 and note.

3 *Artemis*: see *P*.2.7 and note.

67 *Phlegra*: in Thrace.

NEMEAN 2

A short but condensed ode for Timodemus, from Acharnae, a deme of Athens. He had won in the pancration, a violent mixture of boxing and wrestling where only eye-gouging and biting were disallowed. Pindar commemorates victors in this event only in Nemean and Isthmian odes.

1 *the sons of Homer*: singers of Homeric poetry, or rhapsodes, who regarded Homer as their ancestor and customarily prefaced their songs with a prelude to a god; Pindar says here they begin with Zeus simply because of the context, a victory in the Nemean games which were sacred to Zeus. 'Stitched songs' alludes to the etymology of 'rhapsode' as 'song-stitcher'.

11–12 *Orion . . . Pleiades*: an allusive way of saying that Timodemus may, after relatively minor victories at the Nemean, Isthmian, and Pythian games, win the big one at the Olympic games, just as the big constellation of Orion follows the little star-cluster of the Pleiades ('mountain-born' alluding to their father Atlas).

13–14 *Salamis . . . Ajax*: Timodemus, like Ajax son of Telamon, was evidently brought up on the island of Salamis and may have belonged to the Salaminii family on the island who looked after the cult of the hero's son Eurysaces. In the *Iliad*, Ajax generally has the upper hand over Hector, like a pancratiast first knocking him down (7.271), later knocking him out (14.412).

19–21 *Parnassus . . . Pelops . . . Corinth*: at the Pythian and Isthmian games.

NEMEAN 3

Another ode for a pancratiast, this time Aristocleides of Aegina, son of Aristophanes (line 20), whom Pindar compares first with Heracles (lines 22–6), then with Aegina's most famous heroes, Aeacus and his descendants (lines 28–39). The main focus is on Achilles (lines 43–63) because he illustrates the power of inherited natural ability compared with taught skills (see lines 40–2). Aeacus was the son of Zeus and the eponymous nymph Aegina; he and his descendants feature strongly in Pindar's odes for Aeginetan victors. Their family tree looks like this:

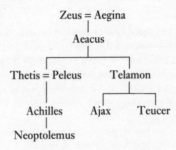

2 *sacred Nemean month*: the Nemean games were held every other year in July.

3 *Dorian*: 'with good old values'; cf. *O*. 8.30.

4 *Asopus'*: a spring on Aegina.

10 *Zeus' daughter*: the Muse Mnemosyne (Memory).

13 *Myrmidons*: early inhabitants of Aegina. The scholiast here quotes from the Hesiodic *Catalogue of Women* (Frag. 205) how Zeus made the Myrmidons from ants (*myrmēkes*) to give Aeacus some companions.

21 *pillars of Heracles*: imagined to be at the Strait of Gibraltar (cf. *N*. 4.69), they stand for the limits of human endeavour. In what follows, Heracles' feats are a heroic analogy to the victor's achievement, but Pindar then turns to the family of Aeacus (line 28) who are more suitable because they are local Aeginetan heroes.

34 *Iolcus*: city in Thessaly; cf. *N*. 4.54–60.

35 *Thetis*: daughter of Nereus (line 57) and difficult to capture because she kept changing shape; cf. *N*. 4.62–5.

37 *Telamon*: son of Aeacus and brother of Peleus; accompanying Heracles and his nephew Iolaus, in a pre-*Iliad* adventure he sacked Troy and killed its king Laomedon and helped get the girdle of the queen of the Amazons, one of Heracles' labours.

43 *Philyra's*: Philyra was mother of the centaur Chiron.

60–1 *Lycians . . . Phrygians . . . Dardanians*: allies of the Trojans.

63 *Memnon*: king of the Ethiopians. His father, Tithonus, and Helenus' father, Priam, were brothers.

69–70 *Apollo's solemn Thearion*: probably a building on Aegina sacred to Apollo, used by Theori, sacred ambassadors who travelled on behalf of the state to the Pythian festival or to consult Apollo's oracle at Delphi. Aristocleides' victory has glorified it, perhaps because of family connections with it or because the ode was performed there.

74 *four virtues*: i.e. four opportunities to excel, as a child, as a man, as an older person, and more generally as a human being who sticks to the task ahead of him.

76 *you*: Aristocleides.

79 *Aeolian*: the precise significance is not known, but, like a number of other similar musical references in the odes (the Lydian, *N.* 4.45, for example), it probably refers to the mode (intervals between notes on the scale).

80 *late*: cf. lines 3–4; the implication is that Pindar's ode was finally performed two years after the victory, but in what follows he suggests that he can make amends, like an eagle which despite coming from afar can swiftly catch its prey.

83 *Cleo*: a Muse, who has inspired Pindar to compose *N.* 3 and thereby helped bathe Aristocleides in glorious light.

84 *Epidaurus . . . Megara*: other places where Aristocleides had won.

NEMEAN 4

An intricate ode that turns and twists from theme to theme as if imitating the twisting and turning of the wrestler for whom it was composed, Timasarchus from Aegina. The mythical section on the Aeacids, Aegina's famous local heroes, focuses on their successes, struggles, and fates, and seems to reflect both the victor's wrestling struggles (see lines 93–4) and the fact that several members of his family mentioned in the course of the ode are now dead (his father Timocritus, line 13, maternal uncle Callicles, line 80, grandfather Euphanes, line 89).

11 *house of the Aeacids*: Aegina.

17 *Cleonae's games*: town near Nemea that organized the Nemean games.

20 *Amphitryon's*: husband of Heracles' mother, Alcmene.

21 *Cadmeians*: Thebans. The 'rich court of Heracles' (line 24) is Thebes itself, the periphrasis motivated by Pindar's wanting to mention Heracles as a means of moving on to the deeds of Aegina's local heroes, the Aeacids (cf. *N.* 3.21–31).

25 *Telamon . . . Troy*: see *N.* 3.36–7, *I.* 6.31–3.

26–7 *Meropes . . . Alcyoneus*: the inhabitants of Cos; a giant.

35 *the wryneck's spell*: a wryneck is 'one or other species of the genus *Iynx* of small migratory scansorial picoid birds; esp. the common species,

Iynx torquilla, distinguished by its habit of writhing the neck and head' (*OED*). The bird was spread on a wheel used in magic spells.

35 *festival of the new moon*: the Nemean games.

36 *deep salt sea . . . waist*: in a mixed metaphor, Pindar imagines that the sea and a wrestling opponent are thwarting his desire to praise the Nemean games; but his praise is all the stronger through having overcome these difficulties. Both images are appropriate, the sea because the victor came from an island, wrestling because he was a wrestler.

45 *Lydian mode*: see note to *N.* 3.79.

46 *Oenone*: old name for Aegina.

46 *Teucer son of Telamon*: grandson of Aeacus, who after the Trojan War went into exile on Cyprus and founded another Salamis there, a magnificent site on the north coast.

48 *Ajax . . . Salamis*: see *N.* 2.13 and note.

49–50 *Achilles . . . Euxine sea*: Achilles was buried on the island of Leuce ('White Island') in the Black Sea (Euxine, 'Friendly', a euphemism, cf. 'Inhospitable' *P.* 4.203).

51 *Phthia*: district in Thessaly where Thetis' husband Peleus lived and Achilles was king.

51–3 *Neoptolemus . . . from Dodona / to the Ionian sea*: Achilles' son Neoptolemus ended up after the Trojan War in Epirus, the region of mainland Greece that contained the famous oracle of Zeus at Dodona and faces the Ionian island of Corfu.

56 *Peleus*: cf. *N.* 3.33–4 and *N.* 5.22–37. Hippolyta, wife of Acastus (son of Pelias, king of Iolcus), persuaded her husband to kill Peleus on the grounds that Peleus had tried to seduce her; Acastus hid Peleus' sword while they went hunting on Mt. Pelion in Thessaly, so he would be easy prey for the centaurs who lived there, but the friendly centaur Chiron saved him. Pindar is adapting Hesiod Frag. 209.

56 *Haemones*: Thessalians.

59 *sword of Daedalus*: Daedalus, the famous Cretan craftsman, is imagined to have made it.

65 *a high-throned Nereid*: Thetis.

69 *Gadeira*: Cadiz; for the idea, cf. *N.* 3.20–1.

73 *Theandridae*: the victor's family clan.

86–7 *Trident-holder's games*: of Poseidon.

93 *Melesias*: Timasarchus' coach. He was a former athlete, and coached other Aeginetans; cf. *O.* 8.54–66, *N.* 6.64–6.

NEMEAN 5

Pytheas, the pancration victor celebrated here, came from a family of Aeginetan fighters. His younger brother Phylacidas won Nemean and

Isthmian victories in the pancration, celebrated by Pindar in *I.* 5 and 6; his maternal uncle Euthymenes won unspecified events at Nemea and elsewhere (lines 41–6); his grandfather Themistius won in the pancration and boxing (lines 50–3). From this and other evidence one can infer that in antiquity there was not the level of event specialization that exists nowadays, and that the pool of talent was relatively small: a strong man could be successful at the games in boxing, wrestling, or pancration. Pytheas' victory was probably in the youths' category (line 6), and was also celebrated by Pindar's rival Bacchylides, who says Pytheas displayed 'exceedingly violent all-fighting strength' (Bacchylides 13.75–6).

8 *Aeacids*: see the family tree in the headnote to *N.* 3.

12 *Endais' famous sons*: Peleus and Telamon were the sons of Endais and Aeacus; they killed their half-brother Phocus, son of Aeacus and Psamatheia, and were forced to leave Aegina (Oenone), Telamon fleeing to Salamis and Peleus to Phthia. According to one account (Apollodorus 3.12.6), Peleus and Telamon were jealous of Phocus' athleticism and killed him while he was training.

10 *father Hellenius*: Zeus Hellenius (Zeus of the Hellenes), who had a sanctuary on Aegina.

22 *these people*: the Aeacids at the wedding of Peleus and Thetis (in Thessaly, where Mt. Pelion stands).

26 *Hippolyta*: for the story see *N.* 4.56–61.

37 *her suitor Poseidon*: Poseidon's wife Amphitrite was, like Thetis, a Nereid.

37 *Aegae*: location uncertain.

43 *the family he shares with that man*: the Aeginetans, regarded as descended from Peleus.

44 *the month that Apollo loves*: a reference to the Delphinian games on Aegina, held in honour of Apollo in the month of Delphinius.

46 *Nisus' hill*: Megara.

48 *Menander's*: Pytheas' coach, who came from Athens.

53 *to Aeacus' temple portico*: to the front of a shrine to Aeacus on Aegina.

NEMEAN 6

This is an unusual ode as it focuses almost entirely on the fluctuating fortunes of the victor's family. Alcimidas, who had won in the boys' wrestling, was a member of the Bassidae clan on Aegina; his victory means that the family, which had already achieved more boxing victories in Greece than any other family (lines 25–6), has now notched up twenty-five victories in the big four games (lines 58–9). But the family has also had its failures, Socleides the victor's great-grandfather having been unsuccessful (lines 20–1), Alcimidas himself and a relative (Polytimidas) missing out at Olympia (lines 62–3), and Alcimidas' father is not mentioned at all, which suggests he had no athletic successes to his credit. The ode is thematically similar to *N.* 11.17–44.

15 *Praxidamas*: he won at Olympia in 544 BC (Pausanias 6.18.7).

21 *Socleides*: father of Praxidamas, great-grandfather of Alcimidas. He was 'greatest of the sons of Hagesimachus' since, although he himself was not victorious, his own three sons were (Praxidamas, and perhaps Callias and Creontidas, lines 36–7).

32 *a cargo of their own praise*: an apposite metaphor, since the Aeginetans were famous as seafarers (cf. *N*. 5.9, etc.).

32 *Pierians' ploughmen*: poets.

37 *offspring of Leto*: Apollo and Artemis.

38 *in the evening*: the cool of the evening was the regular time for celebratory singing; cf. *P*. 11.10.

39 *bridge of the . . . sea*: the Isthmian games.

42–4 *the lion's herb . . . mountains of Phlius*: the Nemean games, where the prize was a garland of fresh celery leaves. Heracles' first labour was to kill the Nemean lion.

49–50b *Ethiopians . . . Memnon . . . Achilles*: cf. *N*. 3.61–3.

62–3 *the lot that was drawn deprived you*: they had an unlucky draw, perhaps because they drew much heavier opponents (as there were no weight divisions). Bacchylides mentions another such incident in connection with a boy wrestler (Bacchylides 11.24–36). The possibility of mismatches, and consequent loss of face for the losers, in the boxing, wrestling, and pancration must have made it difficult for lightweights to succeed, and may underlie *N*. 11.22–9, where a wrestling and pancration victor was prevented by his parents from competing at the Olympian and Pythian games. The comparison that follows between Melesias, famous coach of Aeginetan fighters (mentioned also at *O*. 8.54 and *N*. 4.93 and a dolphin suggests he built up athletes' hand-speed, so that they had a chance against older and heavier opponents.

NEMEAN 7

In contrast with *N*. 6, in this ode no mention is made of previous victories by members of the victor's family, and it is dominated by myth about Neoptolemus, a descendant of Aeacus the great Aeginetan hero and therefore appropriate in an ode for an Aeginetan victor. A scholiast on *N*. 7 (Sch. *N*. 7.150a) says that Aristodemus, a student of the great Alexandrian scholar Aristarchus, believed Pindar's handling of the myth in *N*. 7 was in reaction to criticism of what he had said about Neoptolemus in another poem, *Paean* 6: 'blamed by the Aeginetans for seeming in his *Paeans* to say that Neoptolemus went to Delphi to rob it [intended as a reference to *Paean* 6.118–19], he [Apollo] killed him [Neoptolemus] as he was quarrelling with attendants over countless honours; now it is as if he makes an apology saying that he did not die while temple-robbing but was killed while contesting over sacrificial meat [*N*. 7.42].' A number of modern scholars have followed Aristodemus and believe to varying extents that *N*. 7 does look back to *Paean* 6; all things considered such a view is tenable but disputable (see further on line 33 below, 'as a helper he came'). Pindar's emotive handling of the myth in *N*. 7 may in part be explained by the fact that there was nothing exciting he could say about antecedent victories by the victor or his family.

1–2 *Eleithyia . . . bringer to birth of children*: she is a birth-goddess; there may be a pun involved between her as bringer to birth of children and Sogenes' name which means 'saving the family'.

15 *Mnemosyne*: Memory, mother of the Muses who inspire poets.

17 *Wise men*: they do not come unstuck by a desire for immediate gain but realize the uncertainty of the future, for example that though the sea may be calm now, in the future it may be rough. The 'uncertainty of the future' theme leads Pindar to say that death comes to us all, and the idea that some people have more understanding than others leads to the thought that what Homer says about Odysseus may be exaggerated and in turn to the generalization that poets can deceive and the inability of most people to see the truth.

26 *Ajax*: he killed himself when he failed to win the arms of Achilles.

30 *city of Ilus*: grandfather of Priam; he founded Troy (Ilium).

33 *as a helper he came*: if the text translated (that of the seventh and earlier Teubner editions) is correct, it refers to Neoptolemus' bringing offerings to Delphi (lines 40–1); although he died there in unpleasant circumstances ('in a quarrel', line 42), ultimately he was an honoured hero (cf. lines 31–2, 46–7); the story thus illustrates how posthumous honour can compensate for misfortunes during one's lifetime. Some read 'as a helper I [Pindar] came'. If this reading is correct, it too probably means no more than that Pindar's story about Neoptolemus here restores the hero's good reputation; it could conceivably be taken as a reference to *Paean* 6 and be interpreted as Pindar justifying to the Aeginetans his treatment of Neoptolemus in that poem; but a sudden change of subject to an intervention by Pindar here seems out of place. For another place where he definitely refers to one of his paeans, see headnote to *Isthmian* 1.

37 *Scyros*: the island from where Neoptolemus went to Troy.

37–8 *Ephyra . . . Molossia*: in Epirus, north-west mainland Greece opposite Corfu.

40 *the god*: Apollo. In *Paean* 6 it is Apollo who kills Neoptolemus for having murdered Priam; here Neoptolemus is killed by an unnamed assailant while paying homage to Apollo at Delphi, and his murder of Priam is not mentioned. The change of emphasis could have been motivated by Pindar's desire to present Neoptolemus in a more favourable light following Aeginetan objections to his presentation in the *Paean*.

42 *a man . . . with a knife*: an allusion to Machaereus, son of Daitas, whose name suggests the Greek word for 'knife'.

46–7 *ritual overseer of the processions*: there was probably a cult of Neoptolemus at Delphi.

48–9 *three words will suffice: / it is no lying witness*: 'the above short account will suffice to do justice to Neoptolemus' name; I, Pindar, am a reliable authority for his deeds'; probably a standard break-off formula enabling Pindar to bring the myth to an end (cf. e.g. *N.* 4.33–4, 71–4), possibly alluding to *Paean* 6 and Pindar's wish to set the record straight over Neoptolemus.

64 *No man of Achaea . . . take me to task*: anyone from the land where Neoptolemus lived after the Trojan War (Ephyra on Epirus, 37–8), that is, anyone who supports Neoptolemus, will not find fault with my account. In what immediately follows (lines 66–76), he further stresses its truth.

71 *like a bronze-cheeked javelin*: a metaphor appositely taken from the victor's event, the pentathlon, one of whose disciplines was the javelin-throw. Pindar seems to mean he has not overstepped the mark in what he has said and thereby vitiated it, as an athlete who fouled in the javelin event might disqualify himself from the wrestling that followed.

78–9 *lily-like flower . . . from under the dew of the sea*: coral.

84 *Aeacus*: his mother was the nymph Aegina; his father was Zeus, also father of Heracles.

85 *my famous land*: Pindar adopts the rhetorical strategy of identifying himself with the victor, and, to stress his closeness to the victor (cf. note to *P.* 8.56–60), he claims Aegina is his own homeland.

90 *Subduer of Giants*: cf. *N.* 1.67–9.

94 *his house lies between your precincts*: Sogenes apparently lived in a house between two precincts of Heracles, as a pole goes between the yokes of a four-horse chariot.

96 *grey-eyed daughter*: Athene, daughter of Zeus.

102 *Never will my heart say*: Pindar denies having been unfair to Neoptolemus.

105 *'Corinth belongs to Zeus!'*: a proverbial saying.

NEMEAN 8

This ode is for two Aeginetans, Deinias and his father Megas, each of whom had probably won in the diaulos, a race a length of the stadium and back (lines 16, 48). Megas is dead, but Pindar revives memory of him (lines 44–8), and the myth focuses on the untimely death of Ajax, son of Telamon and grandson of Aeacus.

1 *Hora*: personified beauty of youth.

7 *Cyprian*: Aphrodite.

7 *a son . . . king of Oenone*: Aeacus, king of Aegina.

15 *a Lydian headband patterned with resonant music*: that is, this ode, sung in the Lydian mode, i.e. with Lydian musical harmonies.

18 *Cinyras*: proverbially wealthy king of Cyprus; cf. *P.* 2.15.

19 *I stand here . . . catching my breath before I speak*: like a runner rising up before starting.

26–7 *the Danaans . . . a bloody death*: the story of how Odysseus, not Ajax, won the arms of Achilles and Ajax' consequent suicide is referred to at *N.* 7.25–7.

46 *Chariadae*: the victor's family.

51 *strife arose between Adrastus and the Cadmeans*: the war of the Seven against Thebes; cf. *N.* 9.9–12, and note to *P.* 8.39.

NEMEAN 9

This ode and the two that follow do not celebrate victories in the Nemean games, but post-Pindar Alexandrian scholars placed them as an addendum after the proper Nemean odes because Pindar's *Nemeans* were the last book of his odes in Alexandrian editions and these odes have connections with athletics. This ode is for the same Chromius, a Sicilian general who served under Hieron, as *N.* 1 and commemorates a victory in the chariot race in games at Sicyon, about 20 miles north of Nemea. The ode was composed shortly after the founding of the city of Aetna by Hieron in 476/5 (line 2). The first line of each of the eleven strophes is a hexameter; this gives the ode an air of epic grandeur, suitable for elevating Chromius' noble fighting deeds, and suggests that for the mythical part Pindar may be adapting an epic source. The myth itself (lines 13–27) illustrates the suffering incurred in war and leads Pindar (lines 28–9) to pray that Sicily and Carthage will not come to blows (as they had in 480 when Gelon defeated the Carthaginians at Himera—cf. *P.* 1.72–5).

1 *Apollo's temple at Sicyon*: the games at Sicyon were held in honour of Pythian Apollo (cf. lines 4–5), and founded (according to Pindar) by Adrastus (line 9).

4 *mother and her twin children*: Leto, and Artemis and Apollo.

9 *Asopus*: a river near Sicyon.

14 *Talaus' sons*: Adrastus and his brothers.

17 *son of Oecles*: Amphiaraus.

16 *man-slaying Eriphyle*: Adrastus gave her, his sister, to Amphiaraus to be his wife; this settled the quarrel between Adrastus and Amphiaraus which had led to Adrastus' exile, but Eriphyle was then bribed to force her husband to join the expedition against Thebes and face certain death. For the story of the Seven against Thebes, cf. *P.* 8.39–55.

22 *On the banks of Ismenus*: i.e. at Thebes.

27 *for in god-sent panic even the sons of gods may flee*: therefore Amphiaraus, who had mortal parents, was justified in fleeing Periclymenus.

36 *that goddess*: shame (personified). Pindar means that there was something superhuman about Chromius' sense of shame that spurred him to avoid defeat at all costs.

37 *Enyalius*: Ares, god of war.

40 *Helorus*: river 20 miles south of Syracuse where Chromius distinguished himself in 492 by helping Hippocrates, tyrant of Gela, in a battle against the Syracusans.

51 *silver bowls*: the prize for winning in the games at Sicyon.

NEMEAN 10

A remarkable ode for a man from Argos, Theaeus, son of Oulias (line 24), who for the second time had won the wrestling in the games there in honour of Hera (lines 22–4). He had also won at the Pythian, Nemean, and Isthmian games, among others, and so was keen to gain a victory at the big one, the Olympics, to produce the crowning achievement to complete the set (lines 25–9). Mirroring this pattern—lots of relatively small victories, one big one—is the mythical structure of the ode, which starts with Pindar running through a plethora of myths related to Argos (lines 1–18), and ends with one large myth (lines 55–90) about the Spartan heroes Castor and Polydeuces.

1 *Danaus*: king of Argos, where he had fled from Egypt with his fifty daughters (the Danaids) after they had been forced to marry their cousins; cf. *P*. 9.112–16.

4 *Perseus's encounter . . . Medusa*: see *P*. 12.9–17.

5 *Epaphus*: a king of Egypt and ancestor of Danaus; his mother was Io, a priestess of Hera at Argos, who had fled to Egypt. Many of the following are Io's Argive descendants.

6 *Hypermestra*: Danaid who spared her husband.

7 *Diomedes*: grandson of Adrastus who led from Argos the Seven against Thebes; in the *Iliad* he leads troops from Argos against Troy (2.559–68).

9 *son of Oecles*: Amphiaraus, an Argive, who was one of the Seven against Thebes; cf. *O*. 6.13–14.

11 *Alcmene*: mother of Heracles.

11 *Danae*: mother of Perseus and daughter of Acrisius, king of Argos.

12 *Adrastus' father*: Talaus; cf. *N*. 9.14.

12 *Lynceus*: king of Argos after Danaus.

13 *Amphitryon*: husband of Alcmene. While he was away fighting the Teleboae in Acarnania, Zeus made Alcmene pregnant, whence Heracles.

18 *Hebe*: with the allusion to her mother Hera, goddess of marriage, we return full circle to line 2.

22 *competition for bronze*: at the games for Hera at Argos the prize was a bronze shield, and 100 oxen were sacrificed to the goddess (hence the alternative names for the games, Heraea or Hecatombaea).

25 *Pytho*: the Pythian games.

27 *at the gates to the sea . . . ground established by Adrastus*: further specifications of the Isthmian and Nemean games, the latter regarded as founded by Adrastus.

29 *his heart's true desires*: a victory at the Olympic games ('Pisa', below).

34 *at their rites*: the Panathenaea, where the prize was amphoras of olive oil. A fourth-century inscription says that the winner of the men's stadion there won 100 amphoras of olive oil, about 770 gallons, worth about £25,000 in present-day money. A scholiast here (Sch. *N.* 10.64b) says only victorious athletes could export oil from Athens; this ruling would have allowed them to cash in their oil back home.

39–40 *Thrasyclus or Antias*: relatives of Theaeus on his mother's side, along with Pamphaes (line 49); they had won in various events (cf. lines 48–9) including chariot racing, and hence had been favoured by the Dioscuri ('sons of Tyndareus', line 38), one of whom, Castor, was a great charioteer (cf. *P.* 5.9, *I.* 1.14–17). In return, Pamphaes had hosted a banquet for the Dioscuri (a *theoxenia*, lines 49–50—cf. headnote to *O.* 3).

41–2 *city of Proetus*: Argos. Proetus was twin brother of Danaus and joint king of Argos with him.

42 *Cleonae*: city in charge of the Nemean games.

43 *Sicyon*: see *N.* 9.51 and note.

44 *Pellana*: see *O.* 9.97–8 and note.

45 *bronze*: the prize, in the form of tripods and shields, at various games. Cleitor, Tegea, and Mt. Lycaeon were venues for games in the Peloponnese.

51 *they are natural athletes*: the members of Theaeus' family.

53 *Hermes*: god of athletes, cf. *P.* 2.10, *I.* 1.60.

56 *Therapne*: near Sparta, cf. *P.* 11.61–4. The story that follows is derived from the early Greek epic poem, the *Cypria*. Idas and Lynceus were brothers, sons of Aphareus (line 65).

61 *Taygetus*: mountain-range in Laconia.

61 *Lynceus*: the Lynceus mentioned here and below (line 70) is probably different from the Lynceus mentioned above (line 12).

62 *them*: i.e. Castor and Polydeuces.

66 *Leda's son*: Polydeuces ('Tyndareus son', line 73, although later (lines 80–2) it emerges that only Castor was really the son of Tyndareus).

90 *released*: i.e. brought back to life.

NEMEAN 11

Like the two preceding odes, this does not commemorate a Nemean victory. It honours Aristagoras' becoming a *prytanis* (state official) on the island of Tenedos (in the Aegean near Troy). But Aristagoras had been a victorious wrestler and pancratiast at minor games (line 19) and in Pindar's view might have won at the Pythian and Olympic games (lines 24–9). The overall tone is unusually negative. Bacchylides 14b may also be in honour of an athlete's taking up office.

1 *Hestia*: goddess of the hearth, hence of the official state hearth housed in the *prytaneion* (town hall). Her family connections come from Hesiod (*Theogony* 453–7).

10 *he*: Aristagoras.

11 *Arcesilas*: evidently an athlete like his son.

24–5 *Castalia and Cronus'* . . . *hill*: Delphi and Olympia.

27 *four-year festival* . . . *Heracles*: the Olympic games.

33 *his*: Aristagoras'.

33 *Peisandrus*: an ancestor of Aristagoras; he or his descendants migrated from Amyclae near Sparta to (probably) Lesbos, from where Aeolian settlers colonized nearby Tenedos. Pindar connects this migration with Orestes, who likewise came from Amyclae (cf. *P*. 11.16, 32) and was credited with being responsible for Aeolic migrations. Aristagoras' maternal ancestors came from Thebes (on the river Ismenus), descended from Melanippus, one of the Theban fighters who opposed the Seven against Thebes. So from Orestes and Melanippus Aristagoras had an inborn fighting spirit that helped him as a wrestler and pancratiast.

ISTHMIAN 1

This ode was the subject of an influential study by an American scholar Elroy L. Bundy (*Studia Pindarica*, 2 (Berkeley and Los Angeles, 1986), 35–92) in which he concentrated on Pindar's rhetoric and claimed that the odes were hostile to personal and historical references. The pendulum of Pindaric scholarship, however, has since swung back: the ode is of interest both for what it tells us about Pindar and for reminding us of the importance in general of the historical background for understanding the odes. The victor, Herodotus, had won the chariot race and came from Pindar's own home-city of Thebes. Pindar says that although he is busy working on another poem, a paean to Apollo to be performed on Ceos (perhaps *Paean* 4), he will defer that work out of loyalty to Thebes (1–10); at the end of the poem he hints at the fee he is awaiting from the victor's family (67–8), and in the middle (34–40) alludes to the misfortunes of Herodotus' father, who had probably been exiled from Thebes for fighting on the side of the Persians during the Persian Wars.

1 *Thebe*: eponymous nymph of Thebes.

4 *Delos*: home of Apollo (=Phoebus), about 50 miles east of the island of Ceos which lies off Cape Sounion.

11 *Cadmus' people*: the Thebans.

11 *six crowns*: probably those of Herodotus (line 1) and other Thebans (line 5) in the same Isthmian games (date uncertain).

12 *fearless son*: Heracles. As one of his labours he killed the three-headed monster Geryon who, with his dog(s), kept cattle on an island at the far west of the world. Heracles brought glory to Thebes, his home-city, as did the victor Herodotus.

15 *with his own hands*: usually the victor was not himself the chariot-driver.

29 *Dirce's waters . . . Eurotas*: a spring at Thebes; a river flowing through Sparta.

30 *Iphicles' son*: Iolaus.

30 *Sown Men*: the Thebans, cf. *P.* 9.82.

31 *Tyndareus' son*: Castor, who dwelt at Therapne, overlooking Sparta, among the Achaeans, early inhabitants of the area.

33 *Onchestus' shores*: a Boeotian city, where Poseidon was worshipped, situated between Thebes and Orchomenus (line 35). It seems that Herodotus' father Asopodorus lived in Orchomenus and had land there after his exile from Thebes. If he was the Asopodorus who was a cavalry commander among the Thebans and joined the Persian side at the Battle of Plataea in 479 (Herodotus 9.69), then he may well have had to flee into exile to escape execution (the penalty inflicted on Theban medizers, Herodotus 9.88).

52 *Cronus' son the Earthshaker*: Poseidon, god of horses, the deity presiding over the Isthmian games. There follows the regular list of other places where the victor had won.

55–6 *your sons, Amphitryon*: Heracles and Iolaus, son and grandson of Amphitryon. Both were honoured at Thebes in the games called Heracleia. Strictly speaking, Heracles was the son of Zeus, not Amphitryon.

56 *vale of Minyas*: Orchomenus (see line 35), traditionally associated with a King Minyas.

57 *Eleusis*: at the Eleusinian games.

57 *Euboea's twisting racecourse*: venue uncertain.

58 *Protesilaus*: the first of the Greeks (Achaeans) to land and be killed at Troy. He came from Thessaly where games in his honour were held at Phylace, about 100 miles north of Thebes.

65 *Pierians'*: Muses.

ISTHMIAN 2

Like *P.* 6, this ode ostensibly celebrates a chariot victory by Xenocrates, brother of Theron, tyrant of Acragas in Sicily, for whom Pindar composed *O.* 2 and 3, but it is addressed to his son Thrasybulus, in this case perhaps because Xenocrates had died since the time of his victory.

1–2 *poets of former times*: Pindar contrasts the practice of earlier poets who composed poems for youths they loved with his own practice of writing for money for rich and famous victors. He thereby reminds Thrasybulus that he has the opportunity, by handsomely paying Pindar for this ode, to maintain the generosity (cf. lines 24, 39–42) of his father.

7 *Terpsichore*: one of the Muses.

9–10 *the Argive's saying*: we know nothing about this man from Argos; the saying is mentioned by Alcaeus, too (Frag. 360 *PMG*).

18 *at Crisa*: in the Pythian games.

19 *the Erechtheidae*: Athenians, from their mythical king Erechtheus.

22 *Nicomachus*: unlike Herodotus (see *I.* 1.15), the more eminent Xenocrates did not drive the chariot himself.

23–4 *heralds . . . the Eleans, truce-holders*: prior to the Olympic games, heralds from Elis, where the games were held, declared a sacred truce throughout Greece to allow unhindered passage for participants. Thrasybulus' uncle Theron had won in the chariot race at the Olympics in 476 (for which Pindar composed *O.* 2 and 3) when also Nicomachus was the chariot driver.

28–9 *the sons of Aenesidamus*: Theron and Xenocrates; Xenocrates shares in Theron's Olympic victory.

34 *Heliconian goddesses*: the Muses, who lived on Mt. Helicon.

39 *feast of the gods*: alluding to a *theoxenia* (see headnote to *O.* 3) when a banquet for gods to attend was provided.

41 *Phasis*: a river that goes into the Black Sea. Xenocrates metaphorically travelled to the cooler north in summer, to the hotter south in winter, that is, his generosity knew no bounds and was fitting.

47 *Nicasippus*: the courier for the ode.

ISTHMIANS 3 AND 4

These two poems are for Melissus, son of Telesiadas (*I.* 4.45), of Thebes. It used to be thought in modern times that they formed one single poem, because each is written in the same metre and no other two odes by Pindar are metrically identical with each other, but the presence of some small but important metrical differences make this no longer a popular view. It is also uncertain what victory each ode was composed primarily to celebrate. A possible scenario (M. M. Willcock, *Pindar: Victory Odes* (Cambridge, 1995), 71–2, following G. A. Privitera) is that *I.* 4 was composed first, to celebrate an Isthmian chariot victory (see line 29) but recalling earlier victories of Melissus in the pancration (lines 44–51, 70–2), *I.* 3 subsequently, but before the actual performance of *I.* 4, for both the Isthmian chariot victory and a more recent chariot victory in the Nemean games (lines 11–13). An alternative view (e.g. W. H. Race in his Loeb edition (Cambridge, Mass., and London, 1997), introduction to *I.* 3, p. 154), more in accordance with the emphasis in *I.* 4 itself, regards *I.* 4 as composed to celebrate a single Isthmian pancration victory, though recalling earlier ones too.

ISTHMIAN 3

11–12 *in the low-lying valley of the deep-chested lion*: at Nemea.

15 *Cleonymus*: paternal ancestor of Melissus.

17 *Labdacus' clan*: family of Labdacus, grandfather of Oedipus.

ISTHMIAN 4

See headnote to *I.* 3 and 4 above.

4 *Cleonymids*: see *I.* 3.15 and note.

12 *pillars of Heracles*: marking the limits of human endeavour; cf. *N.* 3.19–21.

17 *cruel snowstorm of war*: possibly the Battle of Plataea (479), when Thebes allied itself with the Persians against the rest of Greece; cf. *I.* 1.34–8.

19 *He who makes the earth tremble, / whose seat is Onchestus*: Poseidon; cf. *I.* 1.33. The 'sea-bridge' is the Isthmus.

24 *Morning Star*: Venus.

26 *Adrastus' games at Sicyon*: cf. *N.* 9.9.

36 *Ajax*: he killed himself after losing out to Odysseus in the competition for the arms of Achilles after Achilles' death; cf. *N.* 7.24–7, *N.* 8.23–7. Since he is introduced as a parallel to Melissus' forebears, the implication is that they failed in the games on a number of occasions in the past.

38 *with his staff*: for the staff which the epic poet held, cf. Hesiod, *Theogony* 30.

49 *Orion*: a giant. The description of Melissus' physique and fighting methods is remarkably detailed and vivid, suggesting that Pindar was personally acquainted with Melissus as a fellow Theban, which in turn perhaps helps to explain how he thought he could get away with the description of him as 'of puny appearance'.

52 *Antaeus*: a Libyan giant, son of Poseidon and Earth.

58 *Aegis-bearer*: Zeus. For the description of Heracles' labours and rewards, see *N.* 1.62–72.

61 *Electran Gates*: one of the seven gates of Thebes. What follows is another detailed description, taken from Pindar's local knowledge, of the Heracleia games at Thebes which included sacrifices and the lighting of fires in memory of Heracles' sons. For Pindar, the sons were warriors ('bronze-armoured', line 63) and he passes over the version of the story, told in Euripides' *Hercules Furens*, in which Heracles himself, made mad by Hera, killed them when they were children.

73 *Orseas*: Melissus' coach.

ISTHMIAN 5

Chronologically, *I.* 5 comes after *I.* 6, *I.* 6 celebrating an Isthmian victory by Phylacidas, a member of the Psalychiadae clan from Aegina, in the pancration as a boy, *I.* 5 an Isthmian victory by him as a man. Phylacidas was the youngest son of Lampon (line 21), and before *I.* 5 and *I.* 6 Pindar had composed one (*N.* 5) for his brother Pytheas, who is praised in *I.* 5 too, not only because of his Nemean victory (lines 20–1; cf. *I.* 6.3–4) but also because he (together with his father, *I.* 6.72–3) coached Phylacidas (lines 59–63). Phylacidas, too, was a Nemean victor (line 18, cf. *I.* 6.61), and other members of the family had also been games victors (*N.* 5.40–6, 50–5; *I.* 6.56–66). So physical prowess ran in the family, and the family is particularly suitable for comparison with the feats of the various members of the Aeacidae. In *I.* 5 Pindar also extols the island of Aegina itself, referring (lines 48–50) to Aegina's part in defeating the Persians at the Battle of Salamis (480), when the Aeginetans suffered losses but distinguished themselves by winning the prize for valour (*aristeia*) (Herodotus 8.93.1, 8.122). In *I.* 6 Pindar's wish that the family might some day celebrate an Olympic victory (*I.* 6.7–9) is expanded in the myth when Zeus fulfils Heracles' wish for a son for Telamon (*I.* 6.43–54).

1   *Theia, mother of the Sun*: as Hesiod, *Theogony* 371. 'Theia' means 'godliness', and Pindar's idea in what follows is that gold and victorious boats, chariots, and athletes are highly valued because they have a divine sun-like splendour.

31 *Oeneus' mighty sons*: Oeneus was king of Calydon in Aetolia (west central Greece), and father of Meleager and Tydeus (father in turn of Diomedes).

34 *Oenone*: old name for Aegina.

36 *twice in battle sacked the city of Troy*: the first time involving Telamon's son Aeacus (cf. *N.* 3.36–7, *N.* 4.24–6, *I.* 6.26–30), the second time Achilles and Neoptolemus, grandson and great-grandson of Aeacus.

38 *lift my gaze up from the plain!*: Pindar invokes the Muse to convey him in her 'chariot of song'.

39–41 *who were Cycnus' killers . . . who Hector's? Memnon's*: all were killed by Achilles; cf. *O.* 2.81–3 and *I.* 8.51–5.

41–2 *Telephus*: king of Mysia in Asia Minor. When his foot got stuck in a vine he was wounded by Achilles en route to Troy (cf. *I.* 8.49–50). The Caicus is a river flowing from Mysia into the Aegean Sea opposite Lesbos.

54 *such as these*: i.e. athletics honours.

55 *Cleonicus*: father of Lampon (cf. *I.* 6.17) and the victor's grandfather.

ISTHMIAN 6

See headnote to *I.* 5.

1   *symposium*: the succession of victories in the games by Lampon's sons (Pytheas, *N.* 5, Phylacidas, *I.* 6, and a hoped-for Olympic victory) is compared to the successive libations at a symposium (to Olympian Zeus, to heroes, to Zeus the saviour).

16 *Cleonicus' son*: Lampon, father of the victor Phylacidas.

17 *Clotho*: see note to *O.* 1.26. She is one of the Fates who map out the course of one's life. Pindar here wants her to map out a future for Lampon that

will agree with his hopes for an Olympic victory by a member of his family.

23 *Nile . . . Hyperboreans*: i.e. worldwide. For the Hyperboreans, a mythical people of the far north, see *P*. 10.30–48.

25 *Peleus*: the father of his wife Thetis was the sea-god Nereus.

30 *Alcmene's son*: Heracles, who, accompanied by Telamon, went from Tiryns (for whose king, Eurystheus, he performed his twelve labours) to Troy (Pergamus) which he destroyed (cf. *N*. 4.24–6) because of the treachery of its king, Laomedon, father of Priam. Laomedon first cheated Apollo and Poseidon of their pay for building Troy's walls for him, and then cheated Heracles of his reward for killing the sea-monster to which Poseidon in his anger had ordered Laomedon to sacrifice his daughter Hesione.

31–3 *Meropes . . . Alcyoneus*: see notes to *N*. 4.26–7.

33 *Phlegrae*: for the battle against the giants on the plains of Phlegra/Phlegrae in Thrace, see *N*. 1.61–9.

35 *Aeacus' son*: Telamon. A scholiast (Sch. *I*. 6.53a) says Pindar in what follows made use of Hesiod's genealogical epic *Greater Catalogue of Women*.

53 *Following the portent of this bird, call him Ajax*: 'the eagle' (*aietos*).

54 *Enyalius*: Ares, god of war.

58 *Euthymenes*: Phylacidas' maternal uncle (line 62); cf. *N*. 5.41–4.

58 *Argive manner*: Argives, like Spartans, were known for their succinctness of expression; cf. *I*. 2.9–11.

65 *Themistius*: Phylacidas' maternal grandfather; cf. *N*. 5.50–4.

67 *Hesiod's maxim*: 'care makes the land prosper' (*Works and Days* 412).

73 *Naxian whetstone*: Naxos, in the Cyclades about 100 miles north of Crete, was noted for its marble and emery.

74 *Dirce*: a spring at Thebes, city of Cadmus.

ISTHMIAN 7

Pindar composed this ode for a fellow Theban, Strepsiades, who had won in the pancration. In it he shows sympathy for Strepsiades' maternal uncle, also called Strepsiades (line 24), who had died in battle, possibly at Oenophyta, about 50 miles east of Thebes, in 457 when Thebes was heavily defeated by Athens; the victory may then have been at the Isthmian games of 454. Though as fighters each Strepsiades met with different fortunes (cf. lines 42–3), nevertheless the glory derived from noble fighting is common to both.

1 *Thebe*: the city of Thebes and its eponymous heroine.

4–5 *Dionysus . . . Demeter*: reference obscure, but evidently referring to a local Theban legend.

5 *at midnight in a snowstorm of gold*: an expression chosen for its suggestions of colours. For Zeus showering gold as a prelude to a birth, cf. *O.* 7.34 (golden snowflakes at Athene's birth), *P.* 12.17 (Perseus).

8 *Teiresias*: Theban prophet.

9 *Iolaus*: Heracles' nephew and charioteer.

10 *the Sown Men*: who sprouted from the dragon's teeth sown by the Theban king Cadmus.

10 *Adrastus*: leader of the disastrous expedition of the Seven against Thebes; see *N.* 9.18–24.

12–15 *Dorian colony . . . Pythian oracles?*: a reference to the 'Dorian invasion' of the Peloponnese; cf. note to *P.* 1.62–6. The Aegeidae were a Theban clan. A scholiast here (18c) cites Aristotle as saying that during the Dorian invasion the Spartans (Lacedaemonians), on the advice of the Pythian oracle, fought with the Aegeidae as allies in their war against neighbouring Amyclae. These quasi-historical connections between Thebes and Sparta, to which Pindar proudly refers elsewhere (*P.* 5.72–6), imbue Thebes with the good old Dorian qualities he so much admired.

31 *son of Diodotus*: Strepsiades the uncle.

32–3 *Meleager . . . Hector . . . Amphiaraus*: heroes who, like Strepsiades the uncle, died in battle.

38 *Earth-holder*: Poseidon, in whose honour the Isthmian games were held.

44–6 *Bellerophon . . . Pegasus*: see on *O.* 13.84–92.

49 *Loxias*: Apollo. Pindar hopes he will in the future be able to celebrate a victory by Strepsiades at the Pythian games too.

ISTHMIAN 8

When in lines 10–11 Pindar says 'Tantalus' stone—an intolerable labour for Hellas— | has been shifted by some god from above our heads', he alludes emotionally to the relief provided by the ending of the Persian Wars (479, at the Battle of Plataea) in which the Aeginetans played a major role (see the headnote to *I.* 5), so the ode can be tentatively dated to the Isthmian games of 478. Parallel to this relief is the relief from toil now due to the victor Cleandrus who fought in the pancration; cf. headnote to *I.* 7 for a similar parallel in that ode. Thebes and Aegina were sisters (lines 16–21), so Pindar as a Theban shares with the victor a natural sympathy at the cost of the defeat of the Persians. In the myth, the glories and death of Achilles take up the theme of the cost of heroism.

10 *Tantalus' stone*: the overhanging stone that formed Tantalus' punishment; see note to *O.* 1.55.

17 *Asopus*: a Boeotian river and its god, father of the twins Thebe and Aegina.

21 *Oenopia's island*: Aegina.

22 *Aeacus*: see the family tree in the headnote to *N.* 3. In saying that he settled disputes for the gods, and (below) that Themis (that is, 'Divine Right') oversaw the marriage of Peleus to Thetis, Pindar emphasizes and praises Aegina's inborn justice (cf. *O.* 8.21–3 'where Themis the Saviour, throned beside Zeus, Protector of Strangers, | is especially honoured among men', *Paean* 6.131, where the island has a 'just regard for foreigners', *I.* 9.5 (a fragment)).

32–3 *a princely son, mightier than his father*: there are several versions of this story (Hesiod, *Theogony* 886–900, [Aeschylus] *Prometheus Bound* 768, 909–10). The *Prometheus* version is closest to Pindar's, but there it is Prometheus himself, not Themis, who delivers the warning; this further suggests that Pindar wanted to give a specially prominent role to Themis in this ode (see previous note).

41 *Chiron's*: he arranged the marriage of Peleus and Thetis, and brought up Achilles (*N.* 3.43–63).

47 *king*: Zeus.

50 *Telephus'*: see note to *I.* 5.41–2.

57 *maidens of Helicon*: the Muses. For their singing on that occasion, see *Odyssey* 24.60–1.

61 *Nicocles*: Cleandrus' cousin (line 66).

67 *Alcathous'*: son of Pelops, for whom games were held at Megara (between Athens and Corinth).

70 *in obscurity*: literally, 'down a hole', an odd expression even for Pindar; the text is uncertain.

Bhagavad Gita

The Bible Authorized King James Version
  With Apocrypha

Dhammapada

Dharmasūtras

The Koran

The Pañcatantra

The Sauptikaparvan (from the
  Mahabharata)

The Tale of Sinuhe and Other Ancient
  Egyptian Poems

The Qur'an

Upaniṣads

ANSELM OF CANTERBURY   The Major Works

THOMAS AQUINAS   Selected Philosophical Writings

AUGUSTINE   The Confessions
On Christian Teaching

BEDE   The Ecclesiastical History

HEMACANDRA   The Lives of the Jain Elders

KĀLIDĀSA   The Recognition of Śakuntalā

MANJHAN   Madhumalati

ŚĀNTIDEVA   The Bodhicaryàvatàra

The Oxford World's Classics Website

www.oup.com/uk/worldsclassics

- Information about new titles
- Explore the full range of Oxford World's Classics
- Links to other literary sites and the main OUP webpage
- Imaginative competitions, with bookish prizes
- Articles by editors
- Extracts from Introductions
- Special information for teachers and lecturers

www.oup.com/uk/worldsclassics